Conveyancing Protocol

Other titles available from Law Society Publishing:

Conveyancing Checklists (3rd edn)
Frances Silverman and Russell Hewitson

Conveyancing Quality Scheme Toolkit (3rd edn)
The Law Society

Conveyancing Handbook (26th edn) (September 2019)
General Editor: Frances Silverman, Consultant Editors: Russell Hewitson, Anne Rodell

Leasehold Enfranchisement and the Right to Manage (3rd edn)
Christopher Sykes

Property Development (3rd edn)
Gavin Le Chat

Residential Conveyancing Practice: A Guide for Support Staff and Paralegals
Russell Hewitson

Risk and Negligence in Property Transactions
Edited by John de Waal QC

Titles from Law Society Publishing can be ordered from all good bookshops or direct (telephone 0370 850 1422 or visit our online shop at **www.lawsociety.org.uk/ bookshop**).

CONVEYANCING PROTOCOL

2019 EDITION

The Law Society

ISBN-13: 978-1-78446-125-6

First edition published in 1990 as *The Law Society's National Conveyancing Protocol: A Guide to the Procedures and Documentation*
Second edition published in 1992
Third edition published in 1994
Fourth edition published in 2001
Fifth edition published in 2005
Sixth edition published in 2011 as *Conveyancing Protocol*

This edition published in 2019 by the Law Society
113 Chancery Lane, London WC2A 1PL

Typeset by Columns Design XML Ltd, Reading
Printed by TJ International Ltd, Padstow, Cornwall

The paper used for the text pages of this book is FSC® certified. FSC (the Forest Stewardship Council®) is an international network to promote responsible management of the world's forests.

FSC
www.fsc.org
MIX
Paper from
responsible sources
FSC® C013056

Contents

Preface

The Law Society introduced the first Conveyancing Protocol (the Protocol) in March 1990. It is the Law Society's preferred practice for transactions that involve the transfer of freehold and leasehold residential properties. Firms that are members of the Law Society's Conveyancing Quality Scheme (CQS) will be expected to follow the procedures set out in the Protocol in so far as this is appropriate for the particular transaction.

The last revision of the Protocol took place simultaneously with the revision of the CQS accreditation to equip conveyancers with best practice methods and procedures.

Practice in conveyancing has moved on since the first Protocol and its last update in 2011. More burden and regulations are imposed on conveyancers and there is a significant increase in the volume of email and the digitisation of various aspects of the procedure. Bearing this in mind, it was obvious that the Protocol needed to be updated. With the introduction of new Core Practice Management Standards, the *Dreamvar* case, SRA regulations surrounding price transparency, government client care recommendations and the revision of the Law Society Code for Completion by Post, now was a perfect opportunity to update the Protocol also.

After careful consideration of the most common complaints to the CQS office, and being aware of the changes in other areas, a small working group, led by the Law Society, was formed to update the Protocol. Although the updated version retains the original intention of setting out the obligations of a conveyancer in a way which assists the client, the group wanted to focus on the additional obligations that solicitors are now under while maintaining the focus and intention to remind conveyancers that lenders are also important clients.

To strengthen the validity of the Protocol, a wide consultation process was implemented to include in its revision input and feedback from, not only the membership, but also external stakeholders.

We continue to urge all firms to join in with the ethos behind the Protocol to ensure that selling or buying a house becomes a less stressful experience for the client. We would also like to invite solicitors to contribute feedback on the experience of using the Protocol so that it may be improved and refined in future editions.

CQS Project Board
June 2019

Acknowledgements

The Law Society would like to thank the following members of the Conveyancing and Land Law Committee and the Residential Property sub-group for their work in drafting the new Protocol and on revising the Code for Completion by Post and the Completion Information and Undertakings form:

- Sarah Dwight
- Mark Sellers
- Hannah Alexander
- Michael Garson
- Laura Ford
- Peter Rodd
- Surekha Gangakhedkar

The Law Society would also like to thank the following members of the Code for Completion Working Party for their contribution to updating the Law Society Code for Completion by Post:

- Philip Freedman CBE QC
- Sarah Dwight
- Nic Taggart
- Warren Gordon
- Laura Ford
- Peter Rodd
- Russell Hewitson
- Mark Sellers
- Stephen Jackson

At the Law Society thanks go to Diane Latter, Andrew Moroney and Victoria Geroe.

The Law Society Conveyancing Protocol

This protocol is known as the Law Society Conveyancing Protocol ('the Protocol').

The Protocol has been designed as the framework for the sale and purchase of a home for an owner occupier. It is assumed that both seller and buyer have lenders and that where a lender is involved it is also a client of the solicitor. It sets out a series of procedures that may be adapted for use in other types of land and property transfers. This Protocol is not intended for use in the purchase of new build homes.

The steps in the Protocol are not exhaustive and should not be regarded as a conveyancing 'checklist'. The transaction may not proceed in a fixed order, and many of the processes can take place simultaneously or be undertaken in a changed order. The use of the Protocol is intended to ensure that all clients are treated fairly and are protected when dealing with high value assets and liabilities. Processes that are open and transparent help make the experience more efficient and reduce wasted time and costs.

PROTOCOL: GENERAL SOLICITOR OBLIGATIONS IN A CONVEYANCING TRANSACTION

The key to reducing stress in a transaction is to manage the client's expectations; to do this you should be taking instructions on matters that could affect the chain (e.g. are parties separating, are they first time buyers, are their circumstances likely to change soon?). It is important to engage proactively with the client when getting your initial instructions. Clients may have been given unrealistic expectations by an estate agent or others about the conveyancing process or the timeframes and they may be unaware of the competing interests; you should engage with those expectations upfront and, where necessary, reset them.

There are many uncertainties in any conveyancing transaction and you cannot be definitive at the beginning of the process. You need to manage your client's expectations at the start and throughout the transaction.

Solicitors are bound by professional obligations to their clients throughout the transaction. A solicitor is required to act in the best interests of each client and those obligations will take precedence over this Protocol.

The following obligations form part of the broader set of obligations of a solicitor and should be undertaken as a matter of course:

1

(a)   To ensure that the transaction can proceed smoothly, you should ensure that all information is shared, subject to any confidentiality obligations that have not been waived.

(b)   Ensure that you have managed and covered timing and other expectations and linked transactions such as chains appropriately.

(c)   Consider any potential conflicts of interest during the whole transaction. These can arise when you are acting for more than one party: sellers, buyers and lenders.

(d)   Ensure that you comply with duties to lenders.

(e)   Act with courtesy and co-operate with third parties.

(f)   Respond promptly particularly in relation to despatch and receipt of money, exchange of contracts and completion.

(g)   Agree at an early stage how you will communicate with all others involved and respond promptly to communications.

(h)   Ensure you always comply with regulatory and statutory requirements and SRA warnings.

(i)   Ensure proper internal and external arrangements for file management have been communicated to your client in relation to holiday and sickness absence.

(j)   Where you are acting for a lender as well as for either the buyer or the seller, the duties owed to the lender client are professional obligations and are subject to the lender client's specific instructions.

(k)   Maintain high standards of courtesy and deal with others in a fair and honest manner.

(l)   Use the most up-to-date version of the Code for Completion by Post, contract, forms and formulae and accompanying guidance published by the Law Society or such approved equivalent publications as may be notified by the Society through periodic updates made on its website at **www.lawsociety. org.uk**. Care should be taken to check the website regularly.

(m)   Ensure you comply with the Money Laundering, Terrorist Financing and Transfer of Funds (Information on the Payer) Regulations 2017 and client identification requirements.

(n)   Ensure that your publicity and costs information (including any website) meets the requirements of the SRA rules and codes of conduct and, to ensure transparency of costs and expenses, ensure you give an accurate estimate to your clients at the time of engagement and adjustments thereafter if relevant.

(o)   Make a record of the advice given to seller, buyer and lender clients at all stages.

(p)   Have regard to the risk management requirements of your professional indemnity insurer.

(q)   Have a continuing awareness of potential cyber security issues.

INTERPRETATION

This section helps with interpretation of the general obligations.

1. Timetable for exchange and completion

Every transaction is different, and the time it may take for each stage in the transaction will be different. Moreover, the timetable that will be expected by the parties at the outset may change and the order in which processes are undertaken may alter. There is no 'normal' transaction and you should communicate this to your clients who need to be made aware that timetables are often set by third parties and the original timetable is no more than a general indication.

2. Transparency

Recognise the value of making the process as transparent as possible. This is likely to assist your clients and help them to be better informed about the process.

3. Lenders

A lender may choose to instruct the conveyancer acting for the seller or the buyer to act on its behalf. Where the lender is a member of UK Finance, the provisions of the UK Finance Mortgage Lenders' Handbook ('Lenders' Handbook') will apply and should be followed (see **www.cml.org.uk/lenders-handbook**). Where a lender is a member of the Building Societies Association (BSA) it may choose to use the BSA Mortgage Instructions. In addition, lenders may have further and additional requirements that alter from time to time.

Lenders who are not members of UK Finance will have their own instructions and requirements which may differ from those in the Lenders' Handbook. Where you are instructed to act for those lenders or to transact through their separate representatives, you should consider the possible impact on timing. You should let those affected know.

If acting solely for the lender, the lender's conveyancer is expected to:

- follow such parts of the Protocol as apply to that retainer; and
- take all action as is necessary to enable both the buyer's conveyancer and the seller's conveyancer to comply with the timescales.

4. Practice points

Solicitors and all their conveyancing staff are expected to:

- consider and stay up to date with all relevant Law Society practice notes (see **www.lawsociety.org.uk**);
- attend regular training to ensure that they remain up to date with law, regulation and best practice.

5. Preferred practice

Use of this Protocol is considered preferred practice. It is only fully effective if both the seller's conveyancer and the buyer's conveyancer adopt it. However, if one party does not agree to adopt it, that does not prevent the use of the procedures by the other party.

PROTOCOL FRAMEWORK

The Protocol sets out a framework for some of the work undertaken.

The seller of a property may be the buyer of another property and likewise the buyer may be the seller of another property. This chain of transactions may be extended by linked transactions. It may be necessary for exchange of contracts to take place simultaneously across the chain. The subsequent completions will usually need to coincide.

Where this occurs, there will be steps that are ascribed in the Protocol to the seller or buyer that the conveyancer will need to be taking at the same time in the mirror transaction in the chain that is linked. Those collateral steps are not set out in the Protocol but need to be considered and applied by conveyancers to ensure that the chain progresses smoothly.

Conveyancers may be instructed at different points in the buying and selling process and therefore the timings in this Protocol can only be indicative. Parties will enter the chain at different times and a chain can only progress as fast or as slow as the slowest member in it and/or the last person to join it.

Where a conveyancer is instructed solely on behalf of the lender and not jointly for both the lender and the borrower then the lender's conveyancer is expected to follow such parts of the Protocol as apply to the retainer and take all action as is necessary to enable both the buyer's conveyancer and the seller's conveyancer to comply with agreed timescales.

Every party will be progressing with their own agenda, which means that agreeing a realistic timetable and reaching final agreement on critical time limits and dates can be challenging. It is important to remember that moving dates or completion dates can only be set credibly and realistically when certain stages have been reached and certain initial requirements fulfilled.

Stage	Steps
A: Instructions	1–9
B: Pre-exchange – submitting a contract	10–19
C: Prior to exchange of contracts	20–21
D: Exchange of contracts	22–27
E: Completion	28–32
F: Post-completion	33–35

STAGE A

Instructions

Contact	Acting for the seller	Acting for the buyer	Contact
1 *Seller* *Agent*	**Client instruction**	**Client instruction**	*Buyer* *Agent*
	Obtain and confirm all instructions and establish the nature of the transaction.	Obtain and confirm all instructions and establish the nature of the transaction.	
	Obtain the agent's commission terms.		
	Send to the seller the Property Information Form (TA6) and Fittings and Contents Form (TA10) (see paragraph (I) of general obligations for further guidance on the use of forms).		
	Linked transactions/chain of transactions	**Linked transactions/chain of transactions**	
	Check whether the seller has property to buy and whether an offer has been accepted and whether there is any linked transaction or chain of transactions. Remember that when you are acting for a seller, you may also be acting for that seller in his capacity as a buyer.	Check whether the buyer has property to sell and whether an offer has been accepted and whether there is any linked transaction or chain of transactions. Remember that when you are acting for a buyer, you may also be acting for that buyer in their capacity as a seller.	

5

Contact	Acting for the seller	Acting for the buyer	Contact
	Occupiers	**Searches**	
	Ascertain the identity of all people aged 17 or over living in the property and consider whether their consent to the sale is required and whether they require independent advice. This may be relevant where they or anyone else may have made any financial contribution towards purchase of the property, mortgage payments, other outgoings or improvements.	Advise the buyer about obtaining searches. Consider which searches would be appropriate to obtain. If so instructed, instigate the searches. If there are two or more buyers, advise on the ways in which property can be owned.	

2 *Seller*	**Regulatory requirements**
	
	Comply with all regulatory requirements (including Transparency Rules):
	
	(1) Provide an estimate of fees and disbursements.
	(2) Provide client care/retainer information and other information required by regulators.
	(3) Provide your terms and conditions.
	(4) Make clients aware of fraud risks and the methods for avoiding them.
	(5) Consider whether other tax advice may be relevant.
		Regulatory requirements
		
		Comply with all regulatory requirements (including Transparency Rules):
		
		(1) Provide an estimate of fees and disbursements.
		(2) Quantify and explain non-optional disbursements:
		   (a) HM Land Registry fees;
		   (b) stamp duty land tax (SDLT), land transaction tax (LTT) including higher rate SDLT/LTT and multiple dwellings relief.
		If you cannot do so, refer the client to your tax department, a tax solicitor or accountant and/or advise your client to take specialist tax advice.
		(3) Explain other disbursements and give estimates, e.g. environmental report.
		(4) Provide client care/retainer information and other information required by regulators.
		(5) Provide your terms and conditions.
			Buyer

6

Contact	Acting for the seller	Acting for the buyer	Contact
		(6) Make clients aware of fraud risks and the methods for avoiding them.	
		(7) Consider whether other tax advice may be relevant.	
3	**Client identity and verification**	**Client identity and verification**	
	Take steps to satisfy yourself and to satisfy any third-party obligation as to the identity of your clients and continue to keep this under review.	Take steps to satisfy yourself and to satisfy any third-party obligation as to the identity of your clients and continue to keep this under review.	
	You should be aware that the buyer's conveyancer will expect you to comply with the undertakings in the Law Society Code for Completion by Post and if you are not able or willing to comply this should be communicated to the buyer's conveyancer at the earliest stage possible.	Satisfy yourself that the seller's conveyancer will give the undertakings for completion in the Law Society Code for Completion by Post which means you do not need to raise further questions at this stage unless there are fraud indicators.	
	Authority to instruct	**Power of attorney**	
	Consider which, if any, documents may need to be signed by an attorney and check whether powers of attorney are available.	Consider which, if any, documents may need to be signed by an attorney and check whether powers of attorney are available.	
	If your client is acting as trustee/executor consider what documents might need to be signed.	Prepare or encourage the buyer to instruct someone to prepare any power that may be necessary.	
	Take steps to satisfy yourself as to the identity of any signatory to contract or transfer so as to be able to satisfy HM Land Registry requirements upon registration.		

Contact	Acting for the seller	Acting for the buyer	Contact
	Obtain instructions for dealing with remittance of gross/net sale proceeds and details provided by the seller of UK bank account for remittance of proceeds. Obtain evidence that the bank account is properly constituted as an account conducted by the seller for a period of at least 12 months. Confirm that remittance will be made to that account only.	**Mortgage requirements**	*Buyer*
Seller	**Mortgage redemption**	Check whether the buyer requires a mortgage offer in connection with any related purchase and, if so, whether:	*Agent*
Agent	Ask the seller how many mortgage accounts need to be redeemed and the approximate amounts outstanding on each account and monthly payment date.	(a) a decision in principle has been obtained;	*Lender/ Broker*
Lender/ Broker		(b) an application has been made; and	
	Obtain redemption figures and advise as to costs of obtaining redemption statements and any later updates and redemption charges.	(c) a mortgage offer has been issued.	
	Check the mortgage or other loans and consider obtaining a statement of account to ascertain redemption penalties or negative equity. If it is apparent that there is negative equity, or for some other reason the seller will not be able to discharge the registered charges from the proceeds of sale, discuss what actions need to be taken.	If a mortgage offer has been made, check that the special conditions can be satisfied.	
		Suggest the buyer consults an independent surveyor for advice on different types of survey and home buyer reports.	
	Advise the seller about continuing to make mortgage payments, ground rent and service charge payments that are due up to and including the completion date.		

Contact	Acting for the seller	Acting for the buyer	Contact
	Restrictions Consider how to deal with any restrictions appearing on the register. **Lender representation** Tell the buyer's conveyancer whether you act for the seller's lender and if not, advise the buyer's conveyancer as to the identity of any solicitor who may be acting for the seller's lender. **Mortgage documentation** If you are not formally instructed by the seller's lender and you are not aware of any conveyancer who has been instructed to act for it, obtain relevant written authority from the seller to deal with the seller's existing lender. Obtain the title deeds, if any and/or ask the seller. In respect of any existing charges entered into by the seller, consider what evidence of discharge or undertakings for discharge are likely to be required by the conveyancers for the buyer's lender and the buyer.	**Lender representation** If you are not to be instructed by the prospective lender, find out who is and check their identity. Suggest the buyer obtains quotations for buildings insurance and advise that the terms of any policy taken out must be compliant with the lender's requirements (where applicable).	
5 *Seller*	**Written confirmation requirements** Ensure the seller has written confirmation of: (a) the name and status of the person who will carry out the work;	**Written confirmation requirements** Ensure the buyer has written confirmation of: (a) the name and status of the person who will carry out the work;	*Buyer*

9

	Contact	Acting for the seller	Acting for the buyer	Contact
		(b) the name of the regulated individual supervising the work;	(b) the name of the regulated individual supervising the work;	
		(c) the complaints procedure; and	(c) the complaints procedure; and	
		(d) cancellation notice where applicable (referring to a cancellation notice if the client decided not to instruct the solicitor).	(d) cancellation notice where applicable (referring to a cancellation notice if the client decided not to instruct the solicitor).	
6	*Seller*	**Costs, checks and payments on account**	**Costs, checks and payments on account**	*Buyer*
		Agree costs estimated and terms for abortive charges.	Agree costs estimated and terms for abortive charges.	
		Carry out and record:	Carry out and record:	
		(a) assessment of transaction risks;	(a) assessment of transaction risk;	
		(b) potential conflicts;	(b) potential conflicts;	
		(c) capacity of client;	(c) capacity of client;	
		(d) scope of authority to act, where there is more than one seller (issues of conflict between them are outside scope – affects remittance of proceeds of sale).	(d) scope of authority to act, where there is more than one buyer (issues of conflict between them are outside scope – affects remittance of proceeds of sale).	
		This obligation continues throughout the transaction.	**This obligation continues throughout the transaction.**	
7		**Title**	**Material information**	*Agent*
		If the title is registered, obtain:	**This obligation continues throughout the transaction.**	*Lender*

Contact	Acting for the seller	Acting for the buyer	Contact
	• up-to-date official copies of the register and title plan;	Review the Memorandum of Sale and/or Property Particulars together with valid energy performance certificate.	
	• official copies of all filed documents;	Explain the likely timescale of the transaction and discuss any factors that may affect it. Keep this under review throughout the transaction.	
	• an official copy of any registered lease; and	Establish the funding requirements.	
	• those documents on which the buyer can reasonably be expected to rely in order to deduce title (e.g. a certified copy of a grant of probate, a power of attorney).	**Potential lender requirements**	
	If the title is unregistered, obtain:	When you know who the lender is, check the Lenders' Handbook Part 2 for information about the lender's requirements.	
	• a land charges search against the seller and any other appropriate names;	As required by the Lenders' Handbook, if you need to report a matter to the lender you must do so as soon as you become aware of it. You should tell the lender what the issue is, identify the relevant provision and provide a summary of the legal risks and your recommendations.	
	• an official search of the index map;		
	• an epitome of title;		
	• those documents on which the buyer can reasonably be expected to rely in order to deduce title (e.g. a certified copy of a grant of probate, a power of attorney).		
	Note: check all plans on copied documents are complete and coloured accurately.		

11

Contact	Acting for the seller	Acting for the buyer	Contact
	Defect in title		
	Consider and advise in relation to any apparent defect in title or missing items in title documents, e.g. missing lease or discrepancies in names or addresses.		
	In some cases, indemnity insurance might be appropriate.		
8 *Seller*	**Leasehold properties**	**Leasehold properties**	*Buyer*
Landlord *Managing agent*	(1) Obtain the lease or official copy of the lease and any deeds of variation.	Ensure that the client is aware of the difference between freehold and leasehold ownership.	*Managing agent*
	(2) Send to the seller a Leasehold Information Form (TA7) in addition to the Property Information Form (TA6) (see paragraph (I) of general obligations for further guidance on the use of forms) and obtain any documents that will be required, including a receipt for ground rent, service charge accounts and insurance details.	Check any lender requirements and report to lender as necessary. Each lender is different, and has its own requirements in relation to leasehold properties.	*Landlord* *Lender*
	(3) Obtain from the seller the contact details for the landlord and/or managing agent and obtain the cost of replies to enquiries in form LPE1 and obtain funds from the seller if required.	Consider the lease and advise the buyer as necessary as soon as you have the information concerning:	
	(4) Consider the lease and advise as necessary concerning the residual lease term.	(a) the residual lease term;	
		(b) the amount of ground rent payable;	
		(c) the method and timing of increases in the ground rent;	
		(d) the amount of service charge payable.	

12

Contact	Acting for the seller	Contact	Acting for the buyer
	(5) Consider timing of submission of LPE1 questions to the landlord/managing agent.		When you have the information provided by the managing agents in response to LPE1, particularly any potential or proposed works to the property which could lead to a substantial increase in the amount of service charge payable, report this to the buyer.
	(6) Consider whether any third parties will need to consent to the sale (e.g. landlord or management company).		
	Continuing obligations		**Continuing obligations**
	Review the costs estimate and revise if necessary, updating information regarding fees or disbursements including managing agent's fees.		Review the costs estimate and revise if necessary, updating information regarding fees or disbursements.
			Consider the timeframe. If the property is leasehold, ensure that the buyer is aware that any enquiries may need to be answered by a third party and adjust the timeframe accordingly.
	Chain of transactions		**Chain of transactions**
9	Consider and advise in relation to any dependent purchase or sale. Advise the seller in relation to their potential tax liability or advise the seller to obtain tax advice as to the order of transactions, where related transactions may not be simultaneous, for SDLT or LTT impact.		Consider and advise in relation to any dependent purchase or sale. Advise the buyer in relation to their potential tax liability or advise the buyer to obtain tax advice as to the order of transactions, where related transactions may not be simultaneous, for SDLT or LTT impact.

13

STAGE B

Pre-exchange – submitting a contract

The seller's conveyancer should generally carry out these steps within five days of confirmation of instructions and submit the draft contract upon receiving confirmation from the buyer's conveyancer that they are instructed.

If there is any delay, explain to the seller, the buyer's conveyancer and the estate agents.

Following acceptance of an offer:

Contact	Acting for the seller	Acting for the buyer	Contact
	Clients' instructions	**Clients' instructions**	
10 *Seller*	Confirm the seller's instructions including checking whether any preliminary deposit or other direct payments have been offered or received. Advise seller not to accept any payment from the buyer.	Confirm the buyer's instructions including checking whether any preliminary deposit or other direct payments have been offered or received. Advise buyer not to accept any payment from the seller or make any payments direct to the seller.	*Buyer* *Lender* *Surveyor*

Contact	Acting for the seller	Acting for the buyer	Contact
	Confirm and update, where necessary, replies to enquiries if completed more than two months earlier.	Advise on liability for SDLT or LTT if you have not already done so. Explain the potential liability for higher rate SDLT/LTT and the circumstances in which this can be reclaimed or advise the buyer.	
		Check availability of deposit.	
		You should advise the buyer that there may be defects in the property which are not revealed by the valuation. You should also advise the borrower to obtain their own survey about the condition of the property.	
		Advise the buyer to investigate the proposed buildings insurance.	
		Where there are two or more people buying a property together, discuss the different types of co-ownership and whether a Declaration of Trust is required.	
	Chain	**Chain**	
	The estate agent should ensure, so far as is possible, that the fullest information is made available as to the status of other transactions in the chain if not provided with the memorandum of sale.	Ensure, so far as is possible, that the fullest information is made available as to the status of other transactions in the chain.	
11	**Conveyancer identification**	**Conveyancer identification**	
	Check the identity of the buyer's conveyancer. Follow the latest SRA and Law Society guidance.	Check the identity of the seller's conveyancer. Follow the latest SRA and Law Society guidance.	

15

Contact	Acting for the seller	Contact	Acting for the buyer	Contact
12	**Confirmation of instructions**		**Confirmation of instructions**	
	Provide the name of the seller, price and other terms agreed. State whether there is any related purchase(s) and extent of chain or any remortgage(s). Inform if seller requires mortgage or any other funding. Inform promptly of any changes.		Provide the name of the buyer, price and other terms agreed. State whether there is any related sale(s) and extent of chain or any remortgage(s). Inform if buyer requires mortgage or any other funding. Inform promptly of any changes.	
	Confirm use of the Protocol and Law Society Code for Completion by Post and expected time required to prepare and submit pre-contract pack of documents.		Confirm use of the Protocol and Law Society Code for Completion by Post. Check details of client bank account.	
	Provide the seller with the information received from the buyer's conveyancer about any related sale by the buyer and any other transactions in the chain and details of the buyer's funding arrangements and mortgage if not previously supplied.		Provide the buyer with the information received from the seller's conveyancer about any related purchase by the seller and any other transactions in the chain.	
13	**Communication**			
	If you intend to email the contract bundle, please tell the buyer's conveyancer that you intend to do so.			
	Delivery of contract bundle by email is acceptable but each document should be a separately identifiable attachment or uploaded individually.			

Contact	Acting for the seller	Acting for the buyer	Contact
	Contract bundle		
	If there is likely to be a delay in submitting a contract bundle, inform the seller, the buyer's conveyancer and the estate agents. So far as possible send the whole package at once.		
	Prepare and submit to the buyer's conveyancer a contract bundle, which includes:		
	(1) The draft contract:		
	(a) incorporating the latest edition of the Standard Conditions of Sale; and		
	(b) only with such additional clauses as are absolutely necessary for the purposes of the transaction; and		
	(c) if appropriate FME1 in relation to service or maintenance charges with accompanying documentation.		
	(2) If the title is registered:		
	(a) up-to-date official copies of the register and title plan;		
	(b) official copies of all filed documents; and		
	(c) those documents on which the buyer can reasonably be expected to rely in order to deduce title (e.g. a certified copy of a grant of probate, a power of attorney, etc.).		

17

Contact	Acting for the seller	Acting for the buyer	Contact
	At the time of submitting the contract bundle, entries in the register of title should be less than six months old. If any information needs to be updated (change of name, death of proprietor) the register should be updated.		
	(3) If the title is unregistered:		
	(a) a land charges search against the seller and any other appropriate names;		
	(b) an official search of the index map;		
	(c) an epitome of title;		
	(d) those documents on which the buyer can reasonably be expected to rely in order to deduce title (e.g. a certified copy of a grant of probate, a power of attorney, etc.).		
	Note: check all plans on copied documents are accurately coloured.		
	(4) Property Information Form (TA6) with supporting documentation. **Note:** copies of competent person certificates are not always required if the existence of the certificate is clear as mentioned in the result of enquiries and noted on the relevant website (such as FENSA).		
	(5) Fittings and Contents Form (TA10).		
	(6) Required consents (e.g. under restrictive covenants or restrictions).		

Contact	Acting for the seller	Acting for the buyer	Contact
	(7) In relation to leasehold property:		
	(a) Leasehold Information Form (TA7);		
	(b) LPE1 in relation to service charge and ground rent with accompanying documentation;		
	(c) official copies of the freehold and intermediate titles;		
	(d) a copy of the seller's share certificate for any landlord/management company where appropriate;		
	(e) draft of any required deed of covenant.		
	Confirm you will complete using the Law Society Code for Completion by Post if you have not already done so. (See paragraph (I) of general obligations for further guidance on the use of forms.)		
	Consider including a draft transfer.		
	Inform the estate agent and the seller when the contract bundle has been submitted.		
	If any document is unavailable or awaited, submit the contract bundle with an explanation as to when it is likely to be supplied.		

19

Contact	Acting for the seller	Acting for the buyer	Contact
14		**Receipt of contract bundle**	*Buyer*
		Notify the buyer that the contract bundle has been received.	
		Notify the seller's conveyancer if expecting to be instructed by the lender or communicate the identity of any other conveyancer instructed by the lender when known.	
		Search requirements	
		If you are not going to make such searches as are required on receipt of the draft contract, notify the seller's conveyancer and provide an indication as to why there may be a delay in submitting searches and when it is likely that they will be submitted.	

	Contact	Acting for the seller	Acting for the buyer	Contact
15	*Agent*	**Additional enquiries**	**Additional enquiries**	
	Seller	Obtain the seller's responses to additional enquiries. Explain that if inappropriate enquiries have been raised, answers need not be given.	**Raise only specific additional enquiries** required to clarify issues arising out of the documents submitted, or which are relevant to the title, existing or planned use, nature or location of the property or which the buyer has expressly requested.	
		Respond to the additional enquiries from the buyer's conveyancer. You do not have to answer inappropriate enquiries.	**Do not raise any additional enquiries** about the state and condition of the building unless arising out of your conveyancing search results, your buyer's own enquiries, inspection or their surveyor's report.	
		The seller should not be required to supply more information than is available in the documents.	**Indiscriminate use of 'standard' additional enquiries may constitute a breach of this Protocol. If such enquiries are submitted, they are not required to be dealt with by the seller/seller's conveyancer.**	
		Inform the seller and the estate agent of any matters likely to delay exchange of contracts.	The seller's conveyancer does not need to obtain the seller's answers to any enquiry seeking opinion rather than fact.	
16	*Seller*	**Fittings and contents**	**Fittings and contents**	*Buyer*
		Take instructions and agree any apportionment of the purchase price in respect of fittings and contents.	Take instructions and agree any apportionment of the purchase price in respect of fittings and contents.	
			Advise the buyer as to the impact of an apportionment of the purchase price for fittings and contents on any mortgage offer and SDLT/LTT.	

Contact	Acting for the seller	Acting for the buyer	Contact
17		**Report to buyer** Report to the buyer on the documentation received and the results of investigations made. **Check title against lender's requirements.** **Draft SDLT/LTT form and signature of documentation.** Prepare (from tax advice received if necessary) a draft online SDLT or LTT return. Consider timing and arrange for signature of any transfer, mortgage deed and SDLT or LTT return. Can be carried out later – see the Lenders' Handbook or the BSA Mortgage Instructions.	
18		**Mortgage instructions** Consider the mortgage instructions from the lender or the lender's conveyancer. Check the mortgage offer conditions with the buyer and if all approved obtain the buyer's signature to the mortgage deed. Consider the instructions from lenders in the Lenders' Handbook or the BSA Mortgage Instructions. If you have reported an issue to the lender, check you have the lender's further written instructions before exchange of contracts because the lender may withdraw or change the mortgage offer.	*Buyer* *Lender*

	Contact	Acting for the seller	Acting for the buyer	Contact
19	*Seller*	**Contract**	**Contract**	*Buyer*
		Deal with any amendments to the contract after taking instructions if necessary.	Approve and return to the seller's conveyancer the draft contract (including the buyer's full name and address) and any necessary amendments.	
		Reply to the Completion Information and Undertakings form (TA13) (see paragraph (I) of general obligations for further guidance on the use of forms).	Submit a draft transfer deed and Completion Information and Undertakings form (TA13) (see paragraph (I) of general obligations for further guidance on the use of forms).	
		Beware how you submit your bank details. It is good practice not to submit bank details by email.		

STAGE C

Prior to exchange of contracts

Contact	Acting for the seller	Acting for the buyer	Contact
20 *Seller*	**Signing of contracts/transfer**	**Signing of contracts/transfer**	*Buyer*
	Report to the seller with the contract for signature (including occupier if relevant) and arrange for the contract to be signed.	Report to the buyer on the purchase documentation and send the contract for signature. Arrange for the contract to be signed and for the buyer to transfer the deposit, preferably electronically.	
	Propose and agree deposit requirements, taking account of any deposit already paid.	Take instructions on the deposit. Agree arrangements for the amount and holding of the deposit where it is to be sent by or held by a third party.	
	Agree the completion date. Ensure the seller is aware of the obligation to give vacant possession by the latest time in the contract (especially if the property is occupied or tenanted).	Take account of any deposit paid under any reservation or pre-contract agreement.	
	Ask the buyer's conveyancer to check the date with others in the buyer's chain to see if it is agreed.	Agree the completion date and time. Ensure that the buyer is aware of the binding nature of the commitment.	
		Check the proposed date with the buyer and the buyer's chain to see if it is agreed. Tell the seller's conveyancer.	

Contact	Acting for the seller	Contact	Acting for the buyer
			Consider the terms on which the deposit is to be held and by whom. Advise the buyer of potential consequences of default if, for example, the deposit is held to order, is less than 10%, or is not held as stakeholder.
21 Seller Managing agent/ Freeholder	**Apportionments** Advise the seller about any apportionments that may be requested in addition to completion monies. Obtain the relevant receipts.	Buyer	**Apportionments** Remind the buyer about the availability of balance of completion monies. Advise as to the date cleared monies are required for completion and any relevant apportionments. Check that the buyer has investigated the availability and cost of buildings insurance, so it is ready to be put in place on exchange or as required by the contract.

25

STAGE D

Exchange of contracts

Contact	Acting for the seller	Acting for the buyer	Contact
22 _Seller_	**Exchange of contracts**	**Exchange of contracts**	_Buyer_
	Use the appropriate Law Society formula for exchange of contracts.	Use the appropriate Law Society formula for exchange of contracts.	
	Notify seller and seller's agent that exchange has taken place immediately after exchange of contracts.	Notify buyer that exchange has taken place immediately after exchange of contracts.	
23	**Completion information and undertakings**	**Completion information and undertakings**	
	Complete TA13 if not already supplied (see paragraph (I) of general obligations for further guidance on the use of forms).	Check replies to TA13 (see paragraph (I) of general obligations for further guidance on the use of forms).	
24	**Transfer**	**Transfer**	
	Provide the buyer's conveyancer with a copy of the transfer executed by the seller, to be delivered on completion.	Check execution of the copy transfer supplied. Consider whether the transfer requires execution by the buyer and whether a duplicate should be signed by the buyer in advance of completion.	
25		**Pre-completion searches**	
		Submit pre-completion searches.	

26

Contact	Acting for the seller	Acting for the buyer	Contact
26 *Lender*	**Redemption figures** Obtain up-to-date redemption figures.		
27		**Certificate of title** Send the certificate of title and/or requisition for funds to the lender (or the lender's conveyancer, if separately represented) promptly.	*Lender*

STAGE E

Completion

Contact	Acting for the seller	Acting for the buyer	Contact
Seller			Buyer
Agent			Lender
28	**Completion procedure**	**Completion procedure**	
	To manage expectations, explain to clients that there are two parts to completion:	To manage expectations, explain to clients that there are two parts to completion:	
	(a) legal completion: involving the transfer of funds and receipt by the seller's conveyancer; and	(a) legal completion: involving the transfer of funds and receipt by the seller's conveyancer; and	
	(b) practical completion: checking the property has vacant possession and is empty, and arrangements for collection of keys by the buyer.	(b) practical completion: checking the property has vacant possession and is empty, and arrangements for collection of keys by the buyer.	
	Explain that these rarely happen simultaneously and that you will let them, or the estate agent, know when the keys can be handed over. This should be no later than the time stated in the contract.	Explain that these rarely happen simultaneously and that you will let them know when completion monies are transferred, and they will need to liaise with the estate agent or the seller as regards the release of keys.	
	On the day before completion, or as early as reasonably possible on the day of completion, consider whether there is likely to be any delay. If there is, notify the buyer's conveyancer and thereafter agree how communication will be handled during the day until completion has taken place.	On the day before completion, or as early as reasonably possible on the day of completion, consider whether there is likely to be any delay. If there is, notify the seller's conveyancer and thereafter agree how communication will be handled during the day until completion has taken place.	

Contact	Acting for the seller	Acting for the buyer	Contact
29	**Completion by post**	**Completion by post**	
	Comply with the Law Society Code for Completion by Post without variation unless there has been prior agreement to vary. General exclusions of liability for obligations within the code will be viewed as a breach of this Protocol in addition to any other consequences.	Comply with the Law Society Code for Completion by Post without variation unless there has been prior agreement to vary. General exclusions of liability for obligations within the code will be viewed as a breach of this Protocol in addition to any other consequences.	
30	**Completion monies and method of completion**	**Completion monies and method of completion**	*Buyer*
Seller			
Agent	On receipt of completion monies, complete the transaction in accordance with the Law Society Code for Completion by Post. This must take place by the latest time stated in the contract. Inform the buyer's conveyancer immediately if this is not possible.	Inform the seller's conveyancer of the commitment of funds to the banking system or instructions given to the bank in accordance with the code.	*Agent*
	Report completion to the seller and proceed with any related purchase.	Report completion of the purchase and the mortgage to the buyer.	
	On completion notify the estate agent and/or any other key holder and authorise release of the keys.	Date and complete the mortgage deed.	
	Date the transfer deed.		
	Send the transfer and any title deeds to the buyer's conveyancer. Send sufficient monies to any lender in accordance with any undertakings.		
31	**Payment of estate agent fees**		
Agent	Pay the estate agent's or property seller's commission, if so authorised.		
Seller			

29

Contact	Acting for the seller	Acting for the buyer	Contact
32 *Seller*	**Outstanding balance of sale proceeds** Account to the seller for any balance of the sale proceeds. Check funds are only being sent to the account details supplied at the beginning of the transaction.		

STAGE F

Post-completion

Contact	Acting for the seller	Acting for the buyer	Contact
33 *Lender*	**Discharge of undertaking** Provide the buyer with sealed Form DS1 (and ID forms where applicable) as soon as it is received and obtain related discharge of undertaking or confirmation as to lodging of END1 by lender if so notified.	**Application to HM Land Registry** Lodge the appropriate SDLT or LTT form with HMRC or the Welsh Revenue Authority as applicable and pay any SDLT/LTT due. Upon receipt of the transfer, lodge your application for registration at HM Land Registry within the priority period of the official search. To reduce the incidence of requisitions being raised by HM Land Registry, check the contents of the application very carefully: ensure that all necessary documents are dated, properly executed and attached and that any name discrepancies between deeds and the register are resolved or explained. Lodge Form DS1 when received (if applicable).	*Lender* *HMRC or Welsh Revenue Authority* *HM Land Registry*
34		**Registration** When registration (whether subject to 'early completion' or not) has been effected: (1) Check the title information document carefully, including the address for service.	*Lender* *Buyer*

31

Contact	Acting for the seller	Acting for the buyer	Contact
		(2) Supply a copy of the title information document to the buyer and remind the buyer to keep the address for service up to date. Advise the client of the existence of the HM Land Registry Property Alert service.	
		(3) Ask the buyer to check the contents of the title information document.	
		(4) Advise the buyer (and any lender) of completion of registration.	
		(5) Deal with any other documents, e.g. mortgage loan agreements, planning permissions, indemnity policies, etc. in accordance with the lender's instructions.	
35 *Seller*	**File closure** Close file after checking and confirm custody of sale contract and sale documents. Return to the client any original documents save for documents which it has been agreed should be retained.	**File closure** Check accounts balance, that addresses are updated, and ledger archived. Return to the client any original documents save for documents which it has been agreed should be retained.	*Buyer*

* Please provide any feedback in relation to the Protocol to **property@lawsociety.org.uk**

A Guide to the Law Society Conveyancing Protocol

1. INTRODUCTION

The Law Society Conveyancing Protocol (the Protocol) is the Law Society's preferred practice for residential conveyancing transactions. It is designed for transactions that involve the transfer of freehold and leasehold residential properties. Firms that are members of the Law Society's Conveyancing Quality Scheme (CQS) will be expected to follow the procedures set out in the Protocol in so far as this is appropriate for the particular transaction.

The first version of the Law Society National Conveyancing Protocol was introduced in March 1990 and it was last updated in 2019. The Protocol is set out in a tabular, rather than a linear, process list form and it is hoped that this will enable clients as well as other professionals involved in the process to understand the stages of the process and what the other party is expected to do at any stage, as well as indicating those points at which contact with others is most likely.

2. THE PROTOCOL

2.1 Date

The Protocol takes effect on 19 August 2019. Some transactions will be part way through at this date and, while the steps in the Protocol that have not already been carried out could be used in these transactions, the use of the Protocol will only be mandatory for CQS members who are commencing a transaction after this date.

2.2 Purpose

This Protocol is designed to bring structure and clarity to communication in residential property transactions.

Some parts of the conveyancing process are not governed by law but are shaped by convention and codes of practice; these develop over time and adapt to meet market practice. The Protocol aims to set out arrangements for the conduct of business between buyers and sellers and their respective solicitors on the basis of a set of agreed principles.

Others involved in the process will be able to better understand the set of processes involved and thereby access information about the stage that a particular transaction has reached. The Protocol can assist in explaining the steps that need to be followed to achieve exchange of contracts and completion of the transaction.

The buying and selling of a home is a non-contentious matter where both parties are broadly looking to achieve the same outcome: that is, the transfer of the home from seller to buyer. Some of the 'general principles' set out at the beginning of the Protocol aim to encompass this fact and to improve communications and reduce unnecessary delays.

Previous iterations of the Protocol have focused on clarifying procedure and practice as between solicitors. This new version incorporates changes in practice and procedure but also faces outwards and aims to provide some transparency. The goal is to enhance the experience for solicitors as well as for the lender and lay clients.

Sellers and buyers are not always familiar with all of the parts of the home buying and selling process. The Protocol is designed to assist solicitors to organise their work where it affects others and to better manage the expectations of sellers and buyers.

The Protocol follows the stages of a typical residential sale and purchase transaction. It does not prescribe the advice that solicitors offer but marshals work into agreed stages. It is hoped that its use will facilitate the interactivity on which the process relies. Where the terms of any transaction make the order of the Protocol inappropriate it is for the users of the Protocol to explicitly agree how they wish to vary the order of the Protocol or agree what alternative steps they wish to adopt.

Typically solicitors instructed by property sellers and buyers will be in contact with estate agents, brokers, lenders and surveyors. It is likely to assist the progress of a transaction if all those involved, including buyers and sellers, know the methodology that solicitors will be adopting in their conduct of the transaction.

2.3   Users

CQS members

The Protocol has been developed and revised as part of the CQS and it is a requirement of the scheme that members follow its obligations. Members must also comply with the Client Service Charter and the Core Practice Management Standards.

CQS accreditation can be applied for by any organisation that is regulated by the Solicitors Regulation Authority (SRA). This will include partnerships, limited liability partnerships, sole practitioners, alternative business structures and incorporated law firms.

CQS members must also achieve the following core values:

- proactively and effectively manage risk and demonstrate behaviours that support and promote the integrity of the CQS and the community;
- demonstrate best practice and excellence in client care through robust practice management of residential conveyancing; and
- demonstrate thorough knowledge and skill in handling conveyancing transactions.

See further **www.lawsociety.org.uk/support-services/accreditation/conveyancing-quality-scheme**.

Those who are not members of the CQS

While it is possible for those who are not CQS members to use the Protocol, it is likely that CQS members will want to carry out checks of non-member firms in order to attempt to establish identity. The status of non-member firms will obviously be especially important in circumstances where professional obligations are involved (for example in relation to the giving of undertakings under the Law Society Code for Completion by Post). In dealing with non-CQS members it will be possible to use the Protocol, but it will not be possible for CQS members to insist that it is used.

The Legal Services Act 2007 makes it an offence to carry on a 'reserved legal activity' through a person who is not entitled so to do. A solicitor should not deal with an unqualified person unless he has clear evidence that no offence under the Legal Services Act 2007 will be committed.

2.4   Scope of the Protocol

The Protocol is designed for use in residential transactions. The Protocol sets out the steps in the most basic of residential transactions. It is for use in freehold and leasehold sales and purchases of residential property. The Protocol is not intended for use in the purchase of new homes.

It is designed to be used in matters that are wholly or primarily residential in nature. In most cases it should be relatively straightforward to establish whether the transaction is residential and one to which the Protocol should apply. However there will be a variety of matters where determination is not so simple. In order to establish whether or not the Protocol applies consider:

- the use of the property;
- the nature of the transaction;
- the nature of the parties;
- the nature of the contract;
- the nature of any mortgage.

Some of these categories may have areas of overlap or may conflict – it will be necessary to decide whether the Protocol should apply to any transaction at its commencement. This should be discussed with the solicitor acting for the other party at the beginning. Even where it is not appropriate to use the Protocol, CQS member firms should still act within the spirit of the Protocol.

2.5   Status of the Protocol

The Protocol has the status of preferred practice.

The Protocol sets out practice standards which are preferred practice and are not regulatory. However, the Protocol does refer to other obligations including legislative, regulatory and other requirements, such as those of mortgage lenders. It is not exhaustive in this regard.

The Protocol contemplates only a very simple transaction and there may be many matters in a transaction that may make some deviation from the Protocol desirable or necessary. It does not include the alternative and additional requirements involved in many kinds of transactions.

This Protocol has been issued by the Law Society for the use and benefit primarily of CQS members. The Protocol sets out the Law Society's view of preferred practice in residential conveyancing. It is not intended to be the only standard of good practice that solicitors can follow.

Where the Protocol refers, for example, to the Code for Completion by Post and the formulae for exchange of contracts, it should be remembered that use of these carries the force of professional obligations.

Solicitors are bound by professional obligations to their clients throughout the transaction. A solicitor must always act in their client's best interests and this obligation will take precedence over the Protocol.

The nature of the transaction, instructions from clients, changes in regulation, statute law or case law may be matters that will take precedence over the Protocol.

It is the responsibility of users of the Protocol to decide when it is appropriate and when it is not appropriate to follow the Protocol. CQS member firms should still act within the spirit of the Protocol if an individual case/circumstance dictates that they need to move away from it.

If the Protocol is not followed in a relevant transaction consideration should be given to how this would be justified to the CQS or to the SRA or other regulatory body. If it is not appropriate to use the Protocol in the context of a particular matter, consider making a note of the explanation for its non-use on file.

If solicitors adopt the Protocol, then they agree to substantially comply with its terms and with the spirit of the process outlined. Any material breach or repeated breaches reported in one or more transactions may result, in the first instance, in the Law Society requiring an explanation from the Senior Responsible Officer (SRO) appointed under the CQS procedures. Repeated cases of serious default will be monitored and where necessary adjudicated under the membership rules of the CQS and may result in expulsion from membership of the CQS.

The Protocol is designed to drive up standards and the quality of work carried out. So, for example, where the contract bundle documents are not checked or are incomplete the seller's solicitor will have failed to meet the standards required if this is not stated and the missing documents are not supplied as soon as reasonably possible.

3. THE GENERAL PRINCIPLES OF THE PROTOCOL

3.1 Overview

The Protocol begins with a list of governing principles that are 'general obligations'.

> (a) To ensure that the transaction can proceed smoothly, you should ensure that all information is shared, subject to any confidentiality obligations that have not been waived.

One of the factors in achieving an uneventful and predictable conveyancing transaction is having good quality communication between all of those involved. This obligation requires that information is shared with others to assist in the efficient management of each transaction or chain of transactions. This only applies in so far as this is permitted by the client. Outcome 4.1 of the SRA Code of Conduct 2011 provides that the affairs of the client must be kept confidential unless, inter alia, the client consents to disclosure. The client is entitled to refuse to permit you to disclose any information and this will outweigh obligations under the Protocol. However, clients should be encouraged only to withhold the authority to disclose in exceptional circumstances.

Transactions are often complicated by the related purchase or sale of another property that must be conducted simultaneously. This position could be replicated a number of times over in a chain of related transactions. Chains will have an impact on the use of the Protocol particularly in relation to timing but will make the principles relating to disclosure even more important. Understanding and taking account of the fact that everyone in the chain is reliant on each other is an important factor in improving the quality of the process. The issue of the provision of information across chains is likely to be the most contentious in the context of confidentiality requirements. The interdependence of transactions arises not only in relation to purchases and sales that depend on one another but in relation to other transactions such as the sale of investments to finance a deposit, the conclusion of a divorce or the issuing of a grant of probate.

The personal circumstances of parties may change unexpectedly or by reason of unemployment, holidays, illness or family events. Problems may arise in the course of a transaction concerning funding, survey, or defects in title. In all of these situations parties will want to be aware of the position as soon as it is known and be clear as to the cause of any delay or breakdown in progress and how long it may take to resolve. The process therefore aims to commit the seller and buyer and their legal advisers to an agreed method of dealing. Those adopting the Protocol will be encouraged to ensure that, where the duty of client confidentiality allows, the timely sharing of information and co-operating with their counterparts leads to enhancement of the client experience and the reduction of time and wasted expenditure.

This is a difficult area – the duty of confidentiality may come into conflict with the requirement for disclosure, but the duty of confidentiality is the paramount obligation (Outcome 4.3 of the SRA Code of Conduct 2011). If the client asks that the seller's agent and solicitor are not told that the client no longer has a buyer for their related sale or has had their mortgage application rejected, then this must take precedence over the obligation to keep everyone informed.

Management of information is as important as the information itself. If the seller is told what the buyer is doing to resolve the problem, they may perhaps be more likely to wait for resolution than they would if they discovered at a later date that the information had been withheld.

(b)   Ensure that you have managed and covered timing and other expectations and linked trans-
       actions such as chains appropriately.

The client may have been given unrealistic expectations by an estate agent or others about the conveyancing process or the timeframes and they may be unaware of competing interests. You should engage with those expectations upfront and, where necessary, reset them.

(c)   Consider any potential conflicts of interest during the whole transaction. These can arise when
       you are acting for more than one party: sellers, buyers and lenders.

Chapter 3 of the SRA Code of Conduct 2011 deals with the proper handling of conflicts of interests. It is important to have in place systems that enable solicitors to identify and deal with potential conflicts.

(d)   Ensure that you comply with duties to lenders.
(e)   Act with courtesy and co-operate with third parties.

The transaction is a non-contentious one. The obligation to act in the best interests of the client is paramount. Consider the main objective of the client in the transaction. The steps of the Protocol should always be followed with care and consideration to all participants.

(f)   Respond promptly particularly in relation to despatch and receipt of money, exchange of
       contracts and completion.

Increased use of electronic communications gives rise to the necessity to agree arrangements for submission of and response to documents. The obligation to submit in duplicate is to counter a growing trend for some firms to submit only one part of the contract and immediately ask their clients to sign the other part. This increases the risk of exchange not being effected in accordance with s.2 of the Law of Property (Miscellaneous Provisions) Act 1989 as the two parts are less likely to be identical.

(g)   Agree at an early stage how you will communicate with all others involved and respond
       promptly to communications.
(h)   Ensure you always comply with regulatory and statutory requirements and SRA warnings.

With a view to avoiding or reducing any unnecessary delay, it is important to respond to all communications promptly. Where something is to be dealt with in a different order or by alternative means this is to be made clear to those who are affected as soon as it is possible to do so. The Protocol recommends that timeframes are agreed where possible.

(i)   Ensure proper internal and external arrangements for file management have been communi-
       cated to your client in relation to holiday and sickness absence.

If the person dealing with the transaction is absent for any reason such absence should be covered by another. The Protocol requires that proper arrangements are put in place for file management.

(j)   Where you are acting for a lender as well as for either the buyer or the seller, the duties owed to
       the lender client are professional obligations and are subject to the lender client's specific
       instructions.

Lenders are important clients and solicitors need to take their instructions very seriously. This is particularly critical in relation to matters that might cause the lender to reconsider its proposals to lend on particular terms, for example in relation to the source of funds over and above the mortgage monies. When you are acting for lender and borrower the duties owed to both clients are equally important.

(k) Maintain high standards of courtesy and deal with others in a fair and honest manner.

Other participants in the process, for example, estate agents, brokers and lenders, have important roles to play. Estate agents may have an understanding of associated transactions and may be able to assist in settling a realistic timetable. A framework for communication with others who may be able to contribute to the process should be considered and addressed in each case at the outset.

(l) Use the most up-to-date version of the Code for Completion by Post, contract, forms and formulae and accompanying guidance published by the Law Society or such approved equivalent publications as may be notified by the Society through periodic updates made on its website at **www.lawsociety.org.uk**. Care should be taken to check the website regularly.

How many firms simply stick to what they know but do not adjust their procedures to take account of changes in practice or in the law? This is a positive obligation to use the most up-to-date versions of forms and to take account of practice materials.

(m) Ensure you comply with the Money Laundering, Terrorist Financing and Transfer of Funds (Information on the Payer) Regulations 2017 and client identification requirements.

Solicitors are the gatekeepers of the process and must endeavour to establish the identities of those they deal with – both clients and those acting on the other side. It is important to be vigilant to guard against fraudulent or any other illegal behaviour by any participant in the conveyancing process. This paragraph is no more than a restatement of obligations but it highlights the importance of these obligations.

(n) Ensure that your publicity and costs information (including any website) meets the require-ments of the SRA rules and codes of conduct and, to ensure transparency of costs and expenses, ensure you give an accurate estimate to your clients at the time of engagement and adjustments thereafter if relevant.

Firms are required to publish information about certain price, service and regulatory matters. See the Law Society's practice note on price and service transparency (**Appendix H4**).

(o) Make a record of the advice given to seller, buyer and lender clients at all stages.
(p) Have regard to the risk management requirements of your professional indemnity insurer.
(q) Have a continuing awareness of potential cyber security issues.

3.2   Interpretation

There is a section in the Protocol about the interpretation of the general obligations. This also demonstrates what is not in the Protocol. The obligations are set out as follows:

1.   Timetable for exchange and completion

Every transaction is different, and the time it may take for each stage in the transaction will be different. Moreover, the timetable that will be expected by the parties at the outset may change and the order in which processes are undertaken may alter. There is no 'normal' transaction and you should communicate this to your clients who need to be made aware that timetables are often set by third parties and the original timetable is no more than a general indication.

This section seeks to encourage the setting of realistic and achievable timetables so that clients know what to expect in terms of timing. The timetable for the transaction is probably one of the most important aspects of the Protocol to the client.

The Protocol sets out a framework for some of the tasks undertaken by the solicitors for the parties. To reduce concerns about delay while the solicitors on each side carry out the work they need to do, consideration should be given to creating a timetable structure for the transaction. For example, allow 10 working days after submission of a contract bundle for each party to report their current position in relation to the timetable for exchange and completion date and to disclose any potential problem or likely delay.

The timing cannot be precise for each stage, but generalised indications are modelled in the Protocol. Where expectations cannot be met it is the responsibility of the solicitor to inform his client and relevant connected parties of the position so that people are kept informed.

2. Transparency

Recognise the value of making the process as transparent as possible. This is likely to assist your clients and help them to be better informed about the process.

3. Lenders

A lender may choose to instruct the conveyancer acting for the seller or the buyer to act on its behalf. Where the lender is a member of UK Finance, the provisions of the UK Finance Mortgage Lenders' Handbook ('Lenders' Handbook') will apply and should be followed (see **www.cml.org.uk/lenders-handbook**). Where a lender is a member of the Building Societies Association (BSA) it may choose to use the BSA Mortgage Instructions. In addition, lenders may have further and additional requirements that alter from time to time.

Lenders who are not members of UK Finance will have their own instructions and requirements which may differ from those in the Lenders' Handbook. Where you are instructed to act for those lenders or to transact through their separate representatives, you should consider the possible impact on timing. You should let those affected know.

If acting solely for the lender, the lender's conveyancer is expected to:

● follow such parts of the Protocol as apply to that retainer; and
● take all action as is necessary to enable both the buyer's conveyancer and the seller's conveyancer to comply with the timescales.

4. Practice points

Solicitors and all their conveyancing staff are expected to:

● consider and stay up to date with all relevant Law Society practice notes (see **www.law society.org.uk**);
● attend regular training to ensure that they remain up to date with law, regulation and best practice.

3.3 Notes

(i) The obligation to act in the best interests of the client takes precedence over the Protocol.
(ii) The steps in the Protocol are not exhaustive and should not be regarded as a conveyancing 'checklist'.
(iii) In some cases the Protocol offers options for a party to adopt according to their preference and in others there is a default position to be followed.
(iv) The Protocol does not set out legal advice and is no substitute for necessary legal advice nor does it set out all the work that needs to be undertaken in order to carry out competently what is required to meet professional and legal obligations.

(v)   The Protocol is a framework for the parties that can be adapted by prior agreement to suit the needs of the parties in any particular situation.

(vi) The seller of a property may be the buyer of another property and likewise the buyer may be the seller of another property. This chain of transactions may be extended by linked transactions. It may be necessary for exchange of contracts to take place simultaneously across the chain. The subsequent completions will usually need to coincide. Where this occurs, there will be steps that are ascribed in the Protocol to the seller or buyer that the conveyancer will need to be taking at the same time in the mirror transaction in the chain that is linked. Those collateral steps are not set out in the Protocol but need to be considered and applied by conveyancers to ensure that the chain progresses smoothly.

(vii) The Protocol does not constitute legal advice, nor does compliance with it necessarily provide a defence to complaints of misconduct or of inadequate professional service. While care has been taken in the drafting of the Protocol the Law Society will not accept any legal liability in relation to it.

3.4   Terms used in the Protocol

(i)   The term 'solicitor' in the context of the Protocol includes solicitors and licensed conveyancers.

(ii)   Terms such as 'seller' and 'buyer' include one person or more than one person.

(iii) 'He' includes 'she'.

(iv) Where reference is made to the UK Finance Mortgage Lenders' Handbook ('Lenders' Handbook'), this only applies where the lender is a full member of UK Finance and instructs using the Lenders' Handbook. Where a lender has elected to instruct under the provisions of the BSA Mortgage Instructions, the Protocol should be read as though referring to the corresponding provisions in the BSA Mortgage Instructions. Where a lender instructs using its own instructions, again the Protocol should be read as though referring to the corresponding provisions in the Lenders' Handbook if appropriate.

4.   OPERATIONAL INFORMATION

4.1   Stage A: Instructions

At this early stage in the process the main steps relate to preparation for later stages.

All regulatory requirements should be complied with, including the SRA Transparency Rules 2018. Also, solicitors should:

- in appropriate cases check the legal capacity of the client in relation to the transaction;
- check there is no conflict of interest that may preclude the solicitor or the firm from acting in the transaction.

Since the earlier versions of the Protocol there are now more obligations in relation to checking the identities of the parties and others in the process and completeness of funding arrangements.

The obligations in relation to checking or attempting to check a client's identity are a regulatory matter rather than a Protocol requirement. Lenders have their own requirements in relation to identity checks to be carried out against borrowers. It is important to keep appropriate records of the checks made in relation to a prospective client's identity. The regulations in this regard are designed to be a precaution against mortgage fraud and money laundering.

For these reasons it is also necessary to check the identity of the solicitor acting for the other side. The Lenders' Handbook provides that lenders are entitled to ask for the details of the other side's regulated legal representatives (as defined by the Legal Services Act 2007, Schedule 4, and Schedule 2, paragraph 5) at the beginning of the transaction.

The Lenders' Handbook also provides that if you are not familiar with the seller's regulated legal representatives, you must verify that they are currently on record with the SRA, Council for Licensed Conveyancers or other legal regulatory body as practising at the address they have provided to you.

In addition to identity it is also important to consider the position of the parties as between themselves particularly when acting for buyers.

Potential lender requirements

When acting for the buyer, once you know who the lender is, you must check Part 2 of the Lenders' Handbook for information about the lender's requirements. As required by the Lenders' Handbook if you need to report a matter to the lender you must do so as soon as you become aware of it. You should tell the lender what the issue is, identify the relevant provision, provide a summary of the legal risks and your recommendations.

Buyers

If a property is being bought by more than one person, the buyers' solicitor will need to take detailed instructions. Buyers should be advised as to the ways in which property can be held in joint names and whether an express declaration of trust should be drawn up. The buyers' solicitor should consider how the beneficial interests will be recorded in the transfer. Whether these are to be recorded by a trust deed or through the transfer itself, the buyers will need to sign the document as a deed. A copy of this should be retained at a later date before application to HM Land Registry for registration. Buyers should be made aware that clarifying these matters at this stage may avoid misunderstandings, cost and expense at a future date or in the event of disagreement as to the nature of the trust.

If there are adults who intend to occupy the property but who will not be owners their consent will be necessary in order to ensure that the lender's rights are binding on them. In this respect it may be appropriate for them to be offered the opportunity to take independent advice.

When acting for a buyer establish whether there will be a sale or mortgage of any other property that will be related to the purchase. If the buyer is in rented accommodation establish the possible termination dates of the tenancy, the period of notice and what arrangements need to be made to give notice.

Sellers and buyers

If there is more than one client, for example where the property is in joint names, it is important to check the scope of the authority to act in this situation. You need to have instructions from both clients even if authority is given for one to act on behalf of them jointly for day-to-day communications.

Sellers

At an early stage the seller's solicitor, if they are not formally instructed by the seller's lender and are not aware of any conveyancer who has been instructed to act for them, should obtain the written authority from the client to deal with the lender authorising the release of any deeds and providing a redemption statement.

Apparent title defects

The obligation on the seller's solicitor, at an early stage in the process, to 'consider and advise in relation to any apparent defect in title or missing items in title documents, e.g. missing lease or discrepancies in names or addresses' aims to assist in accelerating the removal of defects that can cause delays. Management company restrictions, missing evidence of rights of way, mismatching of names of registered proprietors and sellers, need to be investigated or rectified by the seller's solicitor. If the registered title shows entries that will necessitate the transfer being signed by at least two trustees or a trust corporation, this needs to be considered at an early stage. Other matters that can lead to delay include a requirement for the landlord's consent in a leasehold transaction or the use of powers of attorney. If an attorney is involved produce a certified copy of the power at an early stage; remember an attorney must act with at least one other person to overreach beneficial interests in land and that HM Land Registry has detailed identity requirements in relation to attorneys.

Where a client is selling a house, even before a buyer is located, it assists if the seller's solicitor ensures that terms and conditions, identity documents and such like are dealt with. Downloading official copies may reveal that the register needs to be updated – if, for example, a grant of probate needs noting or if there has been a change of name by deed poll or marriage.

Notwithstanding the above, the primary obligation for establishing title remains with the buyer's solicitor and it will remain the obligation of the buyer's solicitor to report on title to his lay client and any lender client.

If the property is leasehold, the seller should supply the information they can about service charges, insurance and ground rent, and make enquiries about the landlord and/or managing agents. The Law Society has produced form LPE1 to obtain information held by a landlord, management companies and managing agents. Sellers will not necessarily wish to put together the full package before the chain is complete, as a result of the cost of doing so and the need to update if finding a buyer takes a long time, but it will assist the process if sufficient information is obtained so that at the minimum it is known where to go and how much it will cost when the need for this information arises. The buyer's solicitor should ensure that the buyer is aware of the difference between freehold and leasehold ownership.

The seller's solicitor may also advise the seller about the desirability of obtaining searches in advance.

4.2   Stage B: Pre-exchange – submitting a contract

This stage involves the collation of the material necessary to provide a bundle of documents for the buyer's solicitor. The steps in this stage should generally be carried out by the seller's solicitor within five days of confirmation of the sale being received. Any delay should be explained to the seller, the buyer's solicitor and the estate agents.

The seller's solicitor should provide as much documentation as is possible at the outset and should, without further prompting from the buyer, apply for and supply filed documents. Official copies should be up to date. This obligation is designed to lessen the possibility of alterations to the register having taken place between production of official copies, submission of papers and pre-completion priority searches.

The obligations in this stage are not wholly prescribed and offer an element of choice. In relation to official copies, these could be obtained by the buyer and it is possible to agree that this will take place. However in circumstances where the seller may give instructions at an early stage, before there is a buyer, requiring the seller's solicitor to obtain the official copies, registered title plan and copies of other registered documents enables them to comply with the requirements to start to address title issues at an early stage.

There is no obligation on sellers to obtain search results for buyers, but they may if they wish. If they do so there is no obligation on a buyer's solicitor to accept such searches.

The seller's solicitor should consider whether to rectify the register to deal with any updating including a change of name on the death of a proprietor. The joint Law Society and HM Land Registry practice note on property and registration fraud (**Appendix H3**) points out that transactions following the death of a registered proprietor are at greater risk from fraudsters posing as executors or the deceased where no note has been made on the register. Updating the register currently carries no application fee.

When the buyer's solicitor receives the contract bundle, the buyer's solicitor is required to notify the seller's solicitor if he is instructed by the buyer's lender or if not to give details of the firm so instructed.

The Protocol requires the seller's solicitor to be satisfied as to the identity of any signatory to the contract or transfer so as to be able to satisfy HM Land Registry's requirements. The seller's solicitor should inform the buyer's solicitor if they are not able to comply with HM Land Registry's requirements for any lender for the purposes of the buyer's application for registration to HM Land Registry (*Practice Guide 67: Evidence of identity; conveyancers*). It is important that these issues are addressed prior to exchange. Even where it is expected that the discharge will be made electronically, if this is not possible it is likely that the discharge will be made by paper DS1 triggering the identification requirements and this will not usually be known until after exchange and sometimes after completion. See the Law Society Code for Completion by Post (**Appendix E**).

Planning permission/building regulations

Sellers are only obliged to provide building regulation documents and planning consents where they themselves have had the work carried out to the property. See Question 4 on the TA6 Property Information Form (**Appendix B1**).

Searches

Following submission of papers, the buyer's solicitor would be expected to request searches, as soon as reasonably possible. If they are to be delayed (for example if the chain of transactions is incomplete), then the seller's solicitor should be notified and provided with an indication as to why there is a delay in submitting the searches and when it is likely that they will be submitted. It is worth noting that some solicitors routinely do not institute searches until the mortgage offer is made available. This may save the buyer money but can lead to delay, so it is important that the seller's solicitor is made aware of this practice as soon as possible.

It is preferred practice for the buyer's solicitor to ensure that the buyer is aware of the limitations of replies to search enquiries.

Enquiries

The buyer's solicitor should raise only those specific additional enquiries that are required to clarify issues arising out of the documents submitted or which are relevant to the title, existing or planned use, particular nature or location of the property or which the buyer has expressly requested.

They should resist raising any additional enquiries about the state and condition of the building unless arising out of their conveyancing search results, the buyer's own enquiries, inspection or surveyor's report. The Protocol includes the longstanding advice of the Law Society as to the type of enquiries to be raised.

It is preferred practice for the buyer's solicitor to ensure that the buyer is aware of the limitations of replies to enquiries and the warranties that should properly be sought.

Purchase price, deposit and incentives

The buyer's and seller's solicitors should advise as to the likely impact on the mortgage offer and the stamp duty land tax (SDLT)/land transaction tax (LTT) liability where apportionment of the purchase price for fittings and contents is suggested. On the information given, is the suggested apportionment plainly unreasonable? Might it affect the percentage being borrowed as lenders will generally only take into account the price paid for the property and not any contents? See **www.hmrc.gov.uk/manuals/sdltmanual/sdltm04010.htm** (SDLT) and **https://beta.gov.wales/chargeable-consideration-technical-guidance** (LTT).

At the present time when there are real constraints on borrowers, with particular problems for first-time buyers obtaining mortgages, many parents, grandparents and others are providing contributions towards the purchase price of the property. Where it becomes apparent that not all of the deposit or purchase monies, other than the mortgage monies, are coming directly from the buyer there are several issues to be considered:

- Does the lender know?
- Is this a matter that should be reported to the lender?
- How is such a contribution to be recorded?
- Should those proposing to advance such monies be advised to first take their own independent advice?

If the property is a new build or new conversion, the buyer's solicitor needs to check with the client to see whether any incentives have been provided by the developer and obtain a UK Finance Disclosure Form completed by or on behalf of the developer from the seller's solicitor. Similar payments may apply in relation to other sales and the client should be asked whether they have received any payment directly from, or made any payment directly to, the other party or intend to do so.

Such matters must be disclosed to the lender.

4.3 Stage C: Prior to exchange of contracts

When the parties are almost ready to exchange it is necessary to check the suggested completion dates with the clients, other solicitors in the chain and, where appropriate, any estate agents.

If there is more than one transaction for a client in a chain, consider the order of exchanging – advise the client of the risks of exchanging on a purchase in advance of exchanging on a sale. The aim is to exchange on both transactions simultaneously, but this is not always possible.

If the deposit is held by the buyer's solicitor 'to the order' of the seller's solicitor, the Protocol requires the parties' solicitors to consider the terms on which it is held.

Usually if no other discussions or communications have taken place, the terms on which the deposit is held might effectively be that an undertaking has been given by the buyer's solicitor that he is holding the deposit in his client account and will send it to the seller's solicitor as soon as this is requested, notwithstanding any argument between the buyer and seller as to legal entitlement to it.

4.4 Stage D: Exchange of contracts

Points to consider

There is the option for the seller's solicitor to deal with the transfer prior to exchange. A solicitor acting for the seller may draft the transfer and obtain the seller's signature to it along with the sale contract in order to reduce the time required between exchange of contracts and completion. If this is done, the seller's solicitor should submit a copy of the executed transfer to the buyer's solicitor in advance in order to ensure that any corrections that may be required are undertaken prior to completion.

Although the obligation is repeated in the Law Society Code for Completion by Post, the seller's solicitor should provide replies to the questions in the TA13 Completion Information and Undertakings form before exchange (see **Appendix B6**). It is common for the buyer's solicitor to send a blank form to the seller's solicitor who rarely completes it but rather sends back a standard word-processed version of the answers, usually adapted with only the identity of the lender and date of the charge to be discharged.

Some firms when acting for sellers submit the TA13 Completion Information and Undertakings form at the outset, but that practice is not recommended by this Protocol. This is mainly because this is likely to result in the undertaking to discharge being given a long time in advance of actual completion when there is a greater possibility of the undertakings being given without full and current information as to the sums involved.

Buyer's and seller's solicitors must both consider the type of discharge that may be given by the lender. This is necessary because identification of the lender will be required in paper discharge cases and it may not be certain that a paper discharge will not be the eventual means of discharge regardless of the information provided before redemption takes place.

Insurance

The buyer's solicitor must advise the buyer of the necessity to commence insurance from the point of exchange as required by the Standard Conditions of Sale (fifth edition – 2018 revision) (see **Appendix C**). The risks of this will need to be explained. The buyer will need to be advised of any requirements that their lender may have in relation to such insurance, including the perils indicated by the lender in its instructions and the minimum sum insured. It will be a useful exercise for the buyer to investigate the insurance terms available for the property they wish to buy well in advance of the likely exchange date. They may learn much about the property from the terms offered by a number of insurers. As flood risk cover becomes ever more important those insurers who have detailed information about flood risk and charge premiums that take this into account may be able to provide useful information to the buyer about the likely risks.

The contract regulates the position concerning who bears the cost of damage to the property if this occurs after exchange. The Protocol requires both the buyer and the seller to be advised by their solicitors about the position relating to insurance. Under the Standard Conditions of Sale the risk of damage passes to the buyer at exchange.

Where the risk in the property has passed to the buyer, the contractual responsibility for any damage becomes that of the buyer. If he or she has insured adequately an insurance claim should produce the amount of the loss allowing completion to take place. However, it is highly unlikely that such funds will be available on completion. This may mean that the contract cannot be completed on the contractual completion date. This may expose the buyer to liability under the contract for late completion.

Even if the buyer has not insured, the Standard Conditions of Sale provide that the buyer must complete the transaction at the contract price. No allowance is to be made for the value of the damage. However, if the payment under the buyer's insurance policy is reduced because the property is also insured by the seller, the Standard Conditions of Sale provide that the purchase price will be reduced by the amount of any reduction. In practice it is likely that some sellers will continue to insure particularly where they have obligations to lenders in this regard.

If the property is damaged before completion, a buyer who is obtaining a mortgage will need the lender's consent to receive the advance. The value of the security may well be reduced and there is a risk that the mortgage offer will be withdrawn. In practice it is suggested that some lenders will be prepared to proceed once an insurance claim has been accepted and arrangements have been put in place for the insurance proceeds to be applied to the rebuilding.

Preparation for completion

In applications to lenders for redemption statements it is suggested that it is made clear to the lender that the seller and the seller's solicitor will be relying on their statement in order to give an undertaking. Asking lenders for statements for all and any charges (and giving all account numbers where possible) that they may have over the property is essential.

The buyer's solicitor needs to consider whether the HM Land Registry early completion policy will apply. He will need to consider the optimum time for carrying out an official search of the register with priority at HM Land Registry. It is suggested this should not be too early, so as to leave the maximum priority period post-completion, and not so late that there is insufficient time for the seller's solicitor to provide any undertakings that will be required if the register has been changed.

The buyer's solicitor should supply the certificate on title and request the mortgage funds and other monies from the client required for completion in good time. Discuss with the buyer/borrower whether the mortgage monies should be requested to arrive the day before completion where the advance is sent by CHAPS, so that completion is not delayed while waiting for the mortgage advance to arrive. Advise the buyer/borrower that they may be charged an additional day's interest.

The day before completion endeavour to establish whether there is likely to be any delay and talk to clients if necessary.

4.5   Stage E: Completion

General

Particularly where clients are physically moving on the day of completion it is important to establish whether there is likely to be any delay in completion and if so to let them know.

In relation to undertakings see particularly the SRA warning notice on undertakings. Note that this was written and issued before the introduction of the SRA Handbook in 2011 and may refer to regulatory material that is no longer in effect.

See also 'Accepting undertakings on completion following the Court of Appeal decision in *Patel* v. *Daybells*' at **Appendix I1**.

There is no obligation to give or accept undertakings and it may be necessary in respect of certain loans and some lenders to consider making arrangements to have the charge discharged in advance of completion. This is particularly relevant in relation to second and third charges.

Undertakings to discharge the seller's mortgage(s)

A reply to the requisition in the TA13 dealing with the discharge of mortgages is treated as an undertaking. Having answered this requisition in the affirmative and given an undertaking to discharge a mortgage the firm is obliged to pay all monies that might be required, even if these exceed the available sale proceeds.

The seller's solicitor should consider whether an undertaking to discharge the seller's mortgage is appropriate at all.

There are risks involved in giving undertakings and steps should be taken to minimise these particularly in relation to situations where there may be 'negative equity' or where 'flexible' mortgage products are involved. Many developers will have given 'all monies' charges and the release of an individual property will necessitate specific agreement between the parties and a signed discharge.

'Offset' or 'flexible' accounts where a current account is linked to a mortgage account are relatively established in the residential mortgage market. Solicitors have used various different methods of establishing a 'fixed' redemption figure in these circumstances.

These have included:

- arranging to retain the proceeds of sale or an amount of funds pending the lender issuing the release;
- requesting the lender to 'freeze' the current account at the point of production of a redemption statement (which is only possible in practical terms where the borrower has access to other current account facilities);
- in circumstances where the bank will not freeze the account, asking the client who then agrees not to use the current account once the redemption statement has been supplied;
- asking the client to provide an additional sum to cover spending on this account prior to completion – some ask the lender for the maximum sum that could be withdrawn from the account in order to establish the maximum liability level – this is then the amount requested from the client.

All of these depend on the relationship the solicitor has with the client and his assessment of the matter generally.

Obviously, there will be matters where solicitors are not able or willing to supply an undertaking on completion and these types of account may feature in a number of such cases. As solicitors should not underwrite the process if it is not reasonable for them to do so it may in some cases be necessary to advise clients to obtain bridging finance. As the process cannot assist consumers in these circumstances it is advisable to give notice of these issues as early as possible in the transaction.

Where an undertaking is to be given the form of the undertaking should be considered by both parties' solicitors.

The undertaking in respect of this discharge is often given under the provisions of the Law Society Code for Completion by Post (the Code). The Protocol requires the buyer's solicitor and the seller's solicitor to adopt the Code without variation unless there has been prior agreement to vary. Standard exclusions of liability for obligations arising under the Code are a breach of the Protocol.

Where the buyer's lender is separately represented and is not represented by the buyer's solicitor it will be necessary to check what form of undertaking for discharge will be required by the solicitor acting for the buyer's lender as well as by the solicitor acting for the buyer. The solicitor acting for the buyer's lender may require that the undertaking be provided directly to them rather than to the buyer's solicitor.

By adopting the Code, the seller's solicitor is under an obligation to send the signed transfer and other agreed documents on the day of completion to the buyer's solicitor.

The seller's solicitor should check that the seller agrees the redemption statement, particularly in relation to penalty or early redemption payments, and advise the seller about mortgage payments that fall due to be paid prior to the completion date.

4.6 Stage F: Post-completion

After completion inform the clients and as necessary the other party's solicitor and the estate agent (for keys) that it has taken place. The seller's solicitor should send the completion documents to the buyer's solicitor under the Code if used. The buyer's solicitor should then file the SDLT/LTT return (the client having previously agreed and signed a hard copy) and pay any SDLT/LTT due. Remember it is the tax return of the client.

Following completion the buyer's solicitor must apply to register the transactions within the priority period of the official search. To reduce the incidence of requisitions being raised by HM Land Registry, the buyer's solicitor should check the contents of the application very carefully and ensure that all necessary documents are dated, properly executed and attached.

The seller's solicitor should provide the buyer's solicitor with the discharge or confirmation that it has been remitted promptly. If the discharge is to take place by form DS1 this needs to be supplied to the buyer's solicitor as soon as it is received. If the lender has discharged any registered charge by electronic means, the seller's solicitor should notify the buyer's solicitor when confirmation is received from the lender. If none is received, the seller's solicitor should contact the lender to obtain such confirmation. When the discharge has been remitted or supplied and the buyer is confident that this has taken place, he can confirm that the undertaking in that respect has been discharged.

There can, as solicitors will be only too well aware, be delays in obtaining evidence of the discharge of the existing charge from some lenders. This may mean HM Land Registry will implement its 'early completion' policy. This allows registration of the purchase and new mortgage to take place even if no notification or documentation relating to the discharged mortgage has been received by HM Land Registry. It is important to apply for registration within the priority period of the search to retain the protection of the search rather than wait for evidence of discharge. Remember that it is not possible to maintain priority by 'renewing' searches. Priority searches cannot be 'renewed'. It is just fortuitous if no other application has been lodged in the meantime. This is the case each time an application is made to 'renew' a priority search. Were all lenders to provide evidence of discharge promptly these issues would largely disappear.

If there is a restriction in the seller's charge that prevents other dispositions being registered, the buyer's solicitor should request that HM Land Registry grant an extension of the time for lodging the discharge to prevent rejection of the application at a later date. Such an extension can usually be requested when HM Land Registry raises requisitions.

When the buyer's solicitor receives the title information document (TID) from HM Land Registry showing the title of the buyer to the property and the lender's interest, they should check its contents including the address(es) for service. A copy should be sent to the buyer, who should be reminded of the benefits of keeping the address(es) for service up to date. The lender should be advised of registration. Lenders have different requirements as to what documents they require following completion, and these will normally be set out in Part 2 of the Lenders' Handbook.

After completion

Post-completion the obligation to provide a discharge continues. Even if the discharge is provided electronically, the seller's solicitor should tell the buyer's solicitor when they are notified by the lender that the discharge has been given. The buyer's solicitor should not wait for evidence of the discharge before applying for registration in an attempt to avoid the application of the early completion procedure. This creates too much risk for the buyer's solicitor. It is not possible to be certain of preserving priority. If another application is made during the currency of the buyer's search by a third party the buyer's solicitor's subsequent search result will be subject to this intervening application. The fact that one might be lucky enough to obtain a further clear search with a new period of priority is not the basis of good practice.

Separate representation

There are sections in the Protocol about separate representation. Many lenders have reduced numbers on their panels to such an extent that some degree of separate representation has been introduced by lenders. The buyer's solicitor should make arrangements as soon as possible to ascertain precisely what will be required by the lender's solicitor and if any change in procedure is required, for example, an undertaking for discharge directly from the seller's solicitor to the lender's solicitor, this should be dealt with as soon as reasonably possible in order to expedite matters, post-exchange.

5. PROTOCOL MATERIALS

5.1 Standard Conditions of Sale (fifth edition – 2018 revision)

When sending out the contract bundle, the seller's solicitor should use the latest edition of the Standard Conditions of Sale and should not add further additional special conditions unless they are absolutely necessary for the purposes of the transaction.

This obligation is designed to stop the multitude of unnecessary special conditions which increase workloads and can militate against co-operation.

Because buyers are often also sellers and sellers are often also buyers the Standard Conditions of Sale are designed to provide a fair balance between the seller and the buyer.

While the Protocol is a form of 'preferred practice' and recommends the use of the Standard Conditions of Sale without amendment where appropriate, the solicitor must use his knowledge and judgement and act in the best interests of the client. It is hoped, however, that the Standard Conditions of Sale will be used with little or no amendment save where absolutely necessary.

5.2 Enquiry forms

The forms that are to be used are set out below.

- Property Information Form (TA6)
  This form raises enquiries commonly requested by buyers. There are difficult areas here in the context of caveat emptor but because many sellers are also buyers the Law Society aims to balance the respective rights of buyers and sellers in the framing of these enquiries. See Explanatory Notes for Sellers and Buyers (**www.lawsociety.org.uk/ support-services/advice/articles/ta6-property-information-form-explanatory- notes**).
- Leasehold Information Form (TA7)
- New Home Information Form (TA8)
- Commonhold Information Form (TA9)
- Fittings and Contents Form (TA10)
  This form sets out those items that are or are not to be included in the sale. It is possible for further sums to be charged for items in addition to the purchase price. This form is to make the position regarding items to be included in the sale clear to buyers and sellers.
  Another aspect of matters relating to these items is the reasonableness of the price for stamp duty land tax/land transaction tax purposes. To agree a figure that is not just and reasonable for the purposes of saving stamp duty land tax/land transaction tax is a criminal offence (**www.hmrc.gov.uk/manuals/sdltmanual/sdltm04010.htm** (SDLT) and **https://beta.gov.wales/chargeable-consideration-technical-guidance** (LTT)).
- Completion Information and Undertakings (TA13)

Solicitors may also use such other equivalents as may be notified by the Law Society from time to time via its website at **www.lawsociety.org.uk**. Solicitors should check the website for regular updates.

5.3 Exchange formulae

The exchange formulae remain A, B and C and these have not changed.

It has always been necessary to record an agreed memorandum of the details of the exchange and any agreed variation of the formula used at the time of the exchange and to retain this in the file. Agreed variations should also be confirmed in writing to the other side. The serious risks of exchanging contracts without a deposit or with a deposit being 'held to order' should be explained to and accepted by the seller client.

The standard form of contract incorporating the Standard Conditions of Sale (fifth edition – 2018 revision) produced by the Law Society and Oyez Professional Services Limited makes provision for a record of the exchange on the front sheet of the contract itself although it does not form part of the contract. Such a record can be extremely important if any question about the exchange were raised subsequently.

As those who effect the exchange will bind their firms or other organisations to the undertakings in the formula used, solicitors should carefully consider who is authorised to effect exchange under the formulae and ensure that use of the procedure is restricted to them. They may also want to ascertain the identity and status of the person with whom they are effecting the exchange. Since professional undertakings form the basis of the formulae they are only recommended for use between solicitors and licensed conveyancers.

5.4   Code for Completion by Post

The Law Society Code for Completion by Post (the Code) provides a voluntary procedure for postal rather than physical completion for residential transactions. It outlines a clear structure for the completion process and clear obligations of sellers' and buyers' solicitors.

The objective of the Code is to provide solicitors with a convenient means for completion on an agency basis when a representative of the buyer's solicitor is not attending at the office of the seller's solicitor.

It may also be used by licensed conveyancers.

It contains important professional obligations and practices will need to ensure that it is dealt with at an appropriate level of seniority within the practice.

Solicitors adopting the Code must be satisfied that its adoption will not be contrary to the interests of their client. When adopted, the Code applies without variation unless otherwise agreed.

To adopt the Code both parties must agree in writing to use the Code to complete a specific transaction except if they have already made it clear that they will be using the Protocol in which case the Code is automatically implied.

The Code has been updated and revised to clarify the position following the Court of Appeal ruling in *P&P Property Ltd* v. *Owen White & Catlin LLP*; *Dreamvar (UK) Ltd* v. *Mishcon De Reya* [2018] EWCA Civ 1082 and solicitors are advised to take note of the contents of the revised Code. The Court of Appeal held that the fraudster seller's solicitor was in breach of the undertaking to the buyer's solicitor implied by the Code, which as properly interpreted required the seller's solicitor to use the completion money for a genuine completion. The changes to the Code make it even clearer that the seller's solicitor is acting in a genuine sale. This should provide innocent buyers with greater protection from fraudsters and help boost consumer confidence in the conveyancing process.

6.   REVIEW OF CONTENT AND CONTACT INFORMATION

Users of the Protocol and supporting documentation are encouraged to provide information as to its operation and content. The Protocol and supporting documentation will be updated regularly.

How to contact us

For queries in relation to membership and other matters relating to CQS contact **CQS@lawsociety.org.uk** or 020 7316 5550.

For queries or comments on the Protocol, the Standard Conditions of Sale, the TA forms, the formulae, the Code or these notes contact **property@lawsociety.org.uk**.

TA6 Property information form (third edition)[1]

Law Society Property Information Form (3rd edition)

Address of the property

Postcode ☐☐☐☐☐☐☐☐

Full names of the seller

Seller's solicitor

Name of solicitor's firm

Address

Email

Reference number

About this form

This form is completed by the seller to supply the detailed information and documents which may be relied upon for the conveyancing process.

It is important that sellers and buyers read the notes below.

Definitions

- 'Seller' means all sellers together where the property is owned by more than one person.
- 'Buyer' means all buyers together where the property is being bought by more than one person.
- 'Property' includes all buildings and land within its boundaries.

The Law Society

TA6

© Law Society 2013

Instructions to the seller

- The answers should be prepared by the person or persons who are named as owner on the deeds or Land Registry title or by the owner's legal representative(s) if selling under a power of attorney or grant of probate or representation. If there is more than one seller, you should prepare the answers together or, if only one seller prepares the form, the other(s) should check the answers given and all sellers should sign the form.

- If you do not know the answer to any question, you must say so. If you are unsure of the meaning of any questions or answers, please ask your solicitor. Completing this form is not mandatory, but omissions or delay in providing some information may delay the sale.

- If you later become aware of any information which would alter any replies you have given, you must inform your solicitor immediately. This is as important as giving the right answers in the first place. Do not change any arrangements concerning the property with anyone (such as a tenant or neighbour) without first consulting your solicitor.

- It is very important that your answers are accurate. If you give incorrect or incomplete information to the buyer (on this form or otherwise in writing or in conversation, whether through your estate agent or solicitor or directly to the buyer), the buyer may make a claim for compensation from you or refuse to complete the purchase.

- You should answer the questions based upon information known to you (or, in the case of legal representatives, you or the owner). You are not expected to have expert knowledge of legal or technical matters, or matters that occurred prior to your ownership of the property.

- Please give your solicitor any letters, agreements or other papers which help answer the questions. If you are aware of any which you are not supplying with the answers, tell your solicitor. If you do not have any documentation you may need to obtain copies at your own expense. Also pass to your solicitor any notices you have received concerning the property and any which arrive at any time before completion of the sale.

Instructions to the buyer

- If the seller gives you, separately from this form, any information concerning the property (in writing or in conversation, whether through an estate agent or solicitor or directly to you) on which you wish to rely when buying the property, you should tell your solicitor.

- You are entitled to rely on the replies given to enquiries but in relation to the physical condition of the property, the replies should not be treated as a substitute for undertaking your own survey or making your own independent enquiries, which you are recommended to do.

- The seller is only obliged to give answers based on their own information. They may not have knowledge of legal or technical matters. You should not expect the seller to have knowledge of, or give information about, matters prior to their ownership of the property.

1 Boundaries

If the property is leasehold this section, or parts of it, may not apply.

1.1 Looking towards the property from the road, who owns or accepts responsibility to maintain or repair the boundary features:

(a) on the left?

☐ Seller ☐ Neighbour
☐ Shared ☐ Not known

(b) on the right?

☐ Seller ☐ Neighbour
☐ Shared ☐ Not known

(c) at the rear?

☐ Seller ☐ Neighbour
☐ Shared ☐ Not known

(d) at the front?

☐ Seller ☐ Neighbour
☐ Shared ☐ Not known

1.2 If the boundaries are irregular please indicate ownership by written description or by reference to a plan:

1.3 Is the seller aware of any boundary feature having been moved in the last 20 years? If Yes, please give details:

☐ Yes ☐ No

1.4 During the seller's ownership, has any land previously forming part of the property been sold or has any adjacent property been purchased? If Yes, please give details:

☐ Yes ☐ No

1.5 Does any part of the property or any building on the property overhang, or project under, the boundary of the neighbouring property or road? If Yes, please give details:

☐ Yes ☐ No

1 Boundaries (continued)

1.6 Has any notice been received under the Party Wall Act 1996 in respect of any shared/party boundaries? If Yes, please supply a copy, and give details of any works carried out or agreed:

☐ Yes   ☐ No
☐ Enclosed   ☐ To follow

2 Disputes and complaints

2.1 Have there been any disputes or complaints regarding this property or a property nearby? If Yes, please give details:

☐ Yes   ☐ No

2.2 Is the seller aware of anything which might lead to a dispute about the property or a property nearby? If Yes, please give details:

☐ Yes   ☐ No

3 Notices and proposals

3.1 Have any notices or correspondence been received or sent (e.g. from or to a neighbour, council or government department), or any negotiations or discussions taken place, which affect the property or a property nearby? If Yes, please give details:

☐ Yes   ☐ No

3.2 Is the seller aware of any proposals to develop property or land nearby, or of any proposals to make alterations to buildings nearby? If Yes, please give details:

☐ Yes   ☐ No

4 Alterations, planning and building control

Note to seller: All relevant approvals and supporting paperwork referred to in section 4 of this form, such as listed building consents, planning permissions, Building Regulations consents and completion certificates should be provided. If the seller has had works carried out the seller should produce the documentation authorising this. Copies may be obtained from the relevant local authority website. Competent Persons Certificates may be obtained from the contractor or the scheme provider (e.g. FENSA or Gas Safe Register). Further information about Competent Persons Certificates can be found at: **www.gov.uk**.

Note to buyer: If any alterations or improvements have been made since the property was last valued for council tax, the sale of the property may trigger a revaluation. This may mean that following completion of the sale, the property will be put into a higher council tax band. Further information about council tax valuation can be found at: **www.voa.gov.uk**.

4.1 Have any of the following changes been made to the whole or any part of the property (including the garden)?

(a) Building works (e.g. extension, loft or garage conversion, removal of internal walls). If Yes, please give details including dates of all work undertaken:
☐ Yes ☐ No

(b) Change of use (e.g. from an office to a residence)
☐ Yes ☐ No
☐ Year

(c) Installation of replacement windows, roof windows, roof lights, glazed doors since 1 April 2002
☐ Yes ☐ No
☐ Year(s)

(d) Addition of a conservatory
☐ Yes ☐ No
☐ Year

4.2 If Yes to any of the questions in 4.1 and if the work was undertaken during the seller's ownership of the property:

(a) please supply copies of the planning permissions, Building Regulations approvals and Completion Certificates, OR:

(b) if none were required, please explain why these were not required – e.g. permitted development rights applied or the work was exempt from Building Regulations:

Further information about permitted development can be found at: **www.planningportal.gov.uk**.

Law Society Property Information Form **TA6**

4 Alterations, planning and building control (continued)

4.3 Are any of the works disclosed in 4.1 above unfinished?
If Yes, please give details:

☐ Yes　　☐ No

4.4 Is the seller aware of any breaches of planning permission conditions or Building Regulations consent conditions, unfinished work or work that does not have all necessary consents? If Yes, please give details:

☐ Yes　　☐ No

4.5 Are there any planning or building control issues to resolve?
If Yes, please give details:

☐ Yes　　☐ No

4.6 Have solar panels been installed?

☐ Yes　　☐ No

If Yes:

(a)　In what year were the solar panels installed?　☐ Year

(b)　Are the solar panels owned outright?　☐ Yes　　☐ No

(c)　Has a long lease of the roof/air space been granted to a solar panel provider? If Yes, please supply copies of the relevant documents.　☐ Yes　　☐ No　☐ Enclosed　☐ To follow

4.7 Is the property or any part of it:

(a)　a listed building?　☐ Yes　　☐ No　☐ Not known

(b)　in a conservation area?　☐ Yes　　☐ No　☐ Not known

If Yes, please supply copies of any relevant documents.　☐ Enclosed　☐ To follow

TA6　*Law Society Property Information Form*　　© Law Society 2013

4 Alterations, planning and building control (continued)

4.8 Are any of the trees on the property subject to a
Tree Preservation Order?

☐ Yes   ☐ No
☐ Not known

If Yes:

(a) Have the terms of the Order been complied with?

☐ Yes   ☐ No
☐ Not known

(b) Please supply a copy of any relevant documents.

☐ Enclosed   ☐ To follow

5 Guarantees and warranties

Note to seller: All available guarantees, warranties and supporting paperwork should be supplied
before exchange of contracts.

Note to buyer: Some guarantees only operate to protect the person who had the work carried out or
may not be valid if their terms have been breached. You may wish to contact the company to establish
whether it is still trading and if so, whether the terms of the guarantee will apply to you.

5.1 Does the property benefit from any of the following guarantees or warranties? If Yes, please
supply a copy.

(a) New home warranty (e.g. NHBC or similar)

☐ Yes   ☐ No
☐ Enclosed   ☐ To follow

(b) Damp proofing

☐ Yes   ☐ No
☐ Enclosed   ☐ To follow

(c) Timber treatment

☐ Yes   ☐ No
☐ Enclosed   ☐ To follow

(d) Windows, roof lights, roof windows or glazed doors

☐ Yes   ☐ No
☐ Enclosed   ☐ To follow

(e) Electrical work

☐ Yes   ☐ No
☐ Enclosed   ☐ To follow

(f) Roofing

☐ Yes   ☐ No
☐ Enclosed   ☐ To follow

Law Society Property Information Form

59

5 **Guarantees and warranties (continued)**

(g) Central heating

☐ Yes   ☐ No
☐ Enclosed   ☐ To follow

(h) Underpinning

☐ Yes   ☐ No
☐ Enclosed   ☐ To follow

(i) Other (please state):

☐ Enclosed   ☐ To follow

5.2 Have any claims been made under any of these guarantees or warranties? If Yes, please give details:

☐ Yes   ☐ No

6 **Insurance**

6.1 Does the seller insure the property?

☐ Yes   ☐ No

6.2 Has any buildings insurance taken out by the seller ever been:

(a) subject to an abnormal rise in premiums?

☐ Yes   ☐ No

(b) subject to high excesses?

☐ Yes   ☐ No

(c) subject to unusual conditions?

☐ Yes   ☐ No

(d) refused?

☐ Yes   ☐ No

If Yes, please give details:

6.3 Has the seller made any buildings insurance claims? If Yes, please give details:

☐ Yes   ☐ No

7 Environmental matters

Flooding

Note: Flooding may take a variety of forms: it may be seasonal or irregular or simply a one-off occurrence. The property does not need to be near a sea or river for flooding to occur. Further information about flooding can be found at: **www.defra.gov.uk**.

7.1 Has any part of the property (whether buildings or surrounding garden or land) ever been flooded? If Yes, please state when the flooding occurred and identify the parts that flooded: ☐ Yes   ☐ No

If No to question 7.1 please continue to 7.3 and do not answer 7.2 below.

7.2 What type of flooding occurred?

(a)	Ground water	☐ Yes	☐ No
(b)	Sewer flooding	☐ Yes	☐ No
(c)	Surface water	☐ Yes	☐ No
(d)	Coastal flooding	☐ Yes	☐ No
(e)	River flooding	☐ Yes	☐ No
(f)	Other (please state):		

7.3 Has a Flood Risk Report been prepared? If Yes, please supply a copy.   ☐ Yes   ☐ No   ☐ Enclosed   ☐ To follow

Further information about the types of flooding and Flood Risk Reports can be found at: **www.environment-agency.gov.uk**.

Radon

Note: Radon is a naturally occurring inert radioactive gas found in the ground. Some parts of England and Wales are more adversely affected by it than others. Remedial action is advised for properties with a test result above the 'recommended action level'. Further information about Radon can be found at: **www.hpa.org.uk**.

7.4 Has a Radon test been carried out on the property?   ☐ Yes   ☐ No

If Yes:

(a)	please supply a copy of the report	☐ Enclosed	☐ To follow
(b)	was the test result below the 'recommended action level'?	☐ Yes	☐ No

© Law Society 2013

Law Society Property Information Form **TA6**

7 Environmental matters (continued)

7.5 Were any remedial measures undertaken on construction to reduce Radon gas levels in the property?

☐ Yes ☐ No ☐ Not known

Energy efficiency

Note: An Energy Performance Certificate (EPC) is a document that gives information about a property's energy usage. Further information about EPCs can be found at: **www.gov.uk**.

7.6 Please supply a copy of the EPC for the property.

☐ Enclosed ☐ To follow ☐ Already supplied

7.7 Have any installations in the property been financed under the Green Deal scheme? If Yes, please give details of all installations and supply a copy of your last electricity bill.

☐ Yes ☐ No ☐ Enclosed ☐ To follow

Further information about the Green Deal can be found at: **www.gov.uk/decc**.

Japanese knotweed

Note: Japanese knotweed is an invasive plant that can cause damage to property. It can take several years to eradicate.

7.8 Is the property affected by Japanese knotweed?

☐ Yes ☐ No ☐ Not known

If Yes, please state whether there is a Japanese knotweed management plan in place and supply a copy.

☐ Yes ☐ No ☐ Not known ☐ Enclosed ☐ To follow

8 Rights and informal arrangements

Note: Rights and arrangements may relate to access or shared use. They may also include leases of less than seven years, rights to mines and minerals, manorial rights, chancel repair and similar matters. If you are uncertain about whether a right or arrangement is covered by this question, please ask your solicitor.

8.1 Does ownership of the property carry a responsibility to contribute towards the cost of any jointly used services, such as maintenance of a private road, a shared driveway, a boundary or drain? If Yes, please give details:

☐ Yes ☐ No

8 Rights and informal arrangements (continued)

8.2 Does the property benefit from any rights or arrangements over any neighbouring property? If Yes, please give details: ☐ Yes ☐ No

8.3 Has anyone taken steps to prevent access to the property, or to complain about or demand payment for access to the property? If Yes, please give details: ☐ Yes ☐ No

8.4 Does the seller know of any of the following rights or arrangements which affect the property?

(a)	Rights of light	☐ Yes	☐ No
(b)	Rights of support from adjoining properties	☐ Yes	☐ No
(c)	Customary rights (e.g. rights deriving from local traditions)	☐ Yes	☐ No
(d)	Other people's rights to mines and minerals under the land	☐ Yes	☐ No
(e)	Chancel repair liability	☐ Yes	☐ No
(f)	Other people's rights to take things from the land (such as timber, hay or fish)	☐ Yes	☐ No

If Yes, please give details:

8.5 Are there any other rights or arrangements affecting the property? If Yes, please give details: ☐ Yes ☐ No

Services crossing the property or neighbouring property

8.6 Do any drains, pipes or wires serving the property cross any neighbour's property? ☐ Yes ☐ No ☐ Not known

8.7 Do any drains, pipes or wires leading to any neighbour's property cross the property? ☐ Yes ☐ No ☐ Not known

Law Society Property Information Form **TA6**

63

8 Rights and informal arrangements (continued)

8.8 Is there any agreement or arrangement about drains, pipes or wires?

☐ Yes ☐ No
☐ Not known

If Yes, please supply a copy or give details:

☐ Enclosed ☐ To follow

9 Parking

9.1 What are the parking arrangements at the property?

9.2 Is the property in a controlled parking zone or within a local authority parking scheme?

☐ Yes ☐ No
☐ Not known

10 Other charges

Note: If the property is leasehold, details of lease expenses such as service charges and ground rent should be set out on the separate TA7 Leasehold Information Form. If the property is freehold, there may still be charges: for example, payments to a management company or for the use of a private drainage system.

10.1 Does the seller have to pay any charges relating to the property (excluding any payments such as council tax, utility charges, etc.), for example payments to a management company? If Yes, please give details:

☐ Yes ☐ No

11 Occupiers

11.1 Does the seller live at the property?

☐ Yes ☐ No

11.2 Does anyone else, aged 17 or over, live at the property?

☐ Yes ☐ No

If No to question 11.2, please continue to section 12 'Services' and do not answer 11.3–11.5 below.

64

11 Occupiers (continued)

11.3 Please give the full names of any occupiers (other than the sellers) aged 17 or over:

11.4 Are any of the occupiers (other than the sellers), aged 17 or over, tenants or lodgers?

☐ Yes   ☐ No

11.5 Is the property being sold with vacant possession?

☐ Yes   ☐ No

If Yes, have all the occupiers aged 17 or over:

(a)   agreed to leave prior to completion?

☐ Yes   ☐ No

(b)   agreed to sign the sale contract? If No, please supply other evidence that the property will be vacant on completion.

☐ Yes   ☐ No
☐ Enclosed   ☐ To follow

12 Services

Note: If the seller does not have a certificate requested below this can be obtained from the relevant Competent Persons Scheme. Further information about Competent Persons Schemes can be found at: **www.gov.uk**.

Electricity

12.1 Has the whole or any part of the electrical installation been tested by a qualified and registered electrician?

☐ Yes   ☐ No

If Yes, please state the year it was tested and provide a copy of the test certificate.

☐ _____ Year
☐ Enclosed   ☐ To follow

12.2 Has the property been rewired or had any electrical installation work carried out since 1 January 2005?

☐ Yes   ☐ No
☐ Not known

If Yes, please supply one of the following:

(a)   a copy of the signed BS7671 Electrical Safety Certificate

☐ Enclosed   ☐ To follow

(b)   the installer's Building Regulations Compliance Certificate

☐ Enclosed   ☐ To follow

(c)   the Building Control Completion Certificate

☐ Enclosed   ☐ To follow

12 Services (continued)

Central heating

12.3 Does the property have a central heating system? ☐ Yes ☐ No

If Yes:

(a) What type of system is it (e.g. mains gas, liquid gas, oil, electricity, etc.)?

```
[                    ]
```

(b) When was the heating system installed? If on or after 1 April 2005 please supply a copy of the 'completion certificate' (e.g. CORGI or Gas Safe Register) or the 'exceptional circumstances' form.

☐ Date
☐ Not known
☐ Enclosed ☐ To follow

(c) Is the heating system in good working order? ☐ Yes ☐ No

(d) In what year was the heating system last serviced/maintained? Please supply a copy of the inspection report.

☐ Year ☐ Not known
☐ Enclosed ☐ To follow
☐ Not available

Drainage and sewerage

Note: Further information about drainage and sewerage can be found at: **www.environment-agency.gov.uk.**

12.4 Is the property connected to mains:

(a) foul water drainage?

☐ Yes ☐ No
☐ Not known

(b) surface water drainage?

☐ Yes ☐ No
☐ Not known

If Yes to both questions in 12.4, please continue to section 13 'Connection to utilities and services' and do not answer 12.5–12.10 below.

12.5 Is sewerage for the property provided by:

(a) a septic tank? ☐ Yes ☐ No

(b) a sewage treatment plant? ☐ Yes ☐ No

(c) cesspool? ☐ Yes ☐ No

12.6 Is the use of the septic tank, sewage treatment plant or cesspool shared with other properties? If Yes, how many properties share the system?

☐ Yes ☐ No
☐ Properties share

12 Services (continued)

12.7 When was the system last emptied? ⬚ Year

12.8 If the property is served by a sewage treatment plant, when was the treatment plant last serviced? ⬚ Year

12.9 When was the system installed? ⬚ Year

Note: Some systems installed after 1 January 1991 require Building Regulations approval, environmental permits or registration. Further information about permits and registration can be found at: **www.environment-agency.gov.uk**.

12.10 Is any part of the septic tank, sewage treatment plant (including any soakaway or outfall) or cesspool, or the access to it, outside the boundary of the property? If Yes, please supply a plan showing the location of the system and how access is obtained.

☐ Yes ☐ No
☐ Enclosed ☐ To follow

13 Connection to utilities and services

Please mark the Yes or No boxes to show which of the following utilities and services are connected to the property and give details of any providers.

Mains electricity Yes ☐ No ☐

Provider's name

Location of meter

Mains gas Yes ☐ No ☐

Provider's name

Location of meter

Mains water Yes ☐ No ☐

Provider's name

Location of stopcock

Location of meter, if any

Mains sewerage Yes ☐ No ☐

Provider's name

Telephone Yes ☐ No ☐

Provider's name

Cable Yes ☐ No ☐

Provider's name

Law Society Property Information Form TA6

14 Transaction information

14.1 Is this sale dependent on the seller completing the purchase of another property on the same day? ☐ Yes ☐ No

14.2 Does the seller have any special requirements about a moving date? If Yes, please give details: ☐ Yes ☐ No

14.3 Does the sale price exceed the amount necessary to repay all mortgages and charges secured on the property? ☐ Yes ☐ No

14.4 Will the seller ensure that:

(a) all rubbish is removed from the property (including from the loft, garden, outbuildings, garages and sheds) and that the property will be left in a clean and tidy condition? ☐ Yes ☐ No

(b) if light fittings are removed, the fittings will be replaced with ceiling rose, flex, bulb holder and bulb? ☐ Yes ☐ No

(c) reasonable care will be taken when removing any other fittings or contents? ☐ Yes ☐ No

(d) keys to all windows and doors and details of alarm codes will be left at the property or with the estate agent? ☐ Yes ☐ No

Signed: .... Dated: ....

Signed: .... Dated: ....

Each seller should sign this form.

The Law Society is the representative body for solicitors in England and Wales.

TA7 Leasehold information form (second edition)[1]

Leasehold Information Form (2nd edition)

Address of the property

Postcode ☐☐☐☐☐☐☐

Full names of the seller

Seller's solicitor

Name of solicitors firm

Address

Email

Reference number

Definitions

- "seller" means all sellers together where the property is owned by more than one person
- "buyer" means all buyers together where the property is being bought by more than one person
- "property" means the leasehold property being sold
- "building" means the building containing the property
- "neighbour" means those occupying flats in the building

Instructions to the seller

The seller should provide all relevant documentation relating to the lease when they return this completed form to their solicitor. This may include documents given to the seller when they purchased the property, or documents subsequently given to the seller by those managing the property.

Instructions to the seller and the buyer

Please read the notes on TA6 Property Information Form

1 The property

1.1 What type of leasehold property does the seller own? ('Flat' includes maisonette and apartment).

◯ Flat
◯ Shared ownership
◯ Long leasehold house

1.2 Does the seller pay rent for the property? If Yes:

◯ Yes   ◯ No

   (a) How much is the current yearly rent?

[＿＿＿＿＿＿＿＿] £

   (b) How regularly is the rent paid (e.g. yearly)?

[＿＿＿＿＿＿＿＿] Payments

2 Relevant documents

2.1 Please supply a copy of:

   (a) the lease and any supplemental deeds

◯ Enclosed   ◯ To follow
◯ Already supplied

   (b) any regulations made by the landlord or by the tenants' management company additional to those in the lease

◯ Enclosed   ◯ To follow
◯ Not applicable

2.2 Please supply a copy of any correspondence from the landlord, the management company and the managing agent.

◯ Enclosed   ◯ To follow

2.3 Please supply a copy of any invoices or demands and any statements and receipts for the payment of:

   (a) maintenance or service charges for the last three years

◯ Enclosed   ◯ To follow
◯ Not applicable

   (b) ground rent for the last three years

◯ Enclosed   ◯ To follow
◯ Not applicable

2.4 Please supply a copy of the buildings insurance policy:

   (a) arranged by the seller and a receipt for payment of the last premium, **or**

◯ Enclosed   ◯ To follow

   (b) arranged by the landlord or management company and the schedule for the current year

◯ Enclosed   ◯ To follow

2.5 Have the tenants formed a management company to manage the building? If Yes, please supply a copy of:

◯ Yes   ◯ No

   (a) the Memorandum and Articles of Association

◯ Enclosed   ◯ To follow

   (b) the share or membership certificate

◯ Enclosed   ◯ To follow

   (c) the company accounts for the past three years

◯ Enclosed   ◯ To follow

3 Management of the building

3.1 Does the landlord employ a managing agent to collect rent or manage the building?

◯ Yes   ◯ No

3.2 Has any management company formed by the tenants been dissolved or struck off the register at Companies House?

◯ Yes   ◯ No
◯ Not known

3.3 Do the tenants pass day to day responsibility for the management of the building to managing agents?

◯ Yes   ◯ No

4 Contact details

4.1 Please supply contact details for the following, where appropriate. (The landlord may be, for example, a private individual, a housing association, or a management company owned by the residents. A managing agent may be employed by the landlord or by the tenants' management company to collect the rent and/or manage the building.)

	Landlord	**Managing agent contracted by the landlord**
Name		
Address		
Tel		
Email		

	Managing agent contracted by the tenants' management company
Name	
Address	
Tel	
Email	

5 Maintenance and service charges

5.1 Who is responsible for arranging the buildings insurance on the property?
- ○ Seller
- ○ Management company
- ○ Landlord

5.2 In what year was the outside of the building last decorated?
[   ] Year ○ Not known

5.3 In what year were any internal communal parts last decorated?
[   ] Year ○ Not known

5.4 Does the seller contribute to the cost of maintaining the building?
○ Yes   ○ No

If No to question 5.4, please continue to section 6 'Notices' and do not answer questions 5.5 – 5.9 below.

5.5 Does the seller know of any expense (e.g. the cost of redecoration of outside or communal areas not usually incurred annually) likely to be shown in the service charge accounts within the next three years? If Yes, please give details:
○ Yes   ○ No

5.6 Does the seller know of any problems in the last three years regarding the level of service charges or with the management? If Yes, please give details:
○ Yes   ○ No

5.7 Has the seller challenged the service charge or any expense in the last three years? If Yes, please give details:
○ Yes   ○ No

5.8 Is the seller aware of any difficulties encountered in collecting the service charges from other flat owners? If Yes, please give details:
○ Yes   ○ No

APPENDIX B2

5.9 Does the seller owe any service charges, rent, insurance premium or other financial contribution? If Yes, please give details:

☐ Yes   ☐ No

6 Notices

Note: a notice may be in a printed form or in the form of a letter.

6.1 Has the seller received a notice that the landlord wants to sell the building? If Yes, please supply a copy.

☐ Yes   ☐ No
☐ Enclosed   ☐ To follow
☐ Lost

6.2 Has the seller received any other notice about the building, its use, its condition or its repair and maintenance? If Yes, please supply a copy.

☐ Yes   ☐ No
☐ Enclosed   ☐ To follow
☐ Lost

7 Consents

Note: A consent may be given in a formal document, a letter or orally.

7.1 Is the seller aware of any changes in the terms of the lease or of the landlord giving any consents under the lease? If Yes, please supply a copy or, if not in writing, please give details:

☐ Yes   ☐ No
☐ Enclosed   ☐ To follow
☐ Lost

8 Complaints

8.1 Has the seller received any complaint from the landlord, the management company or any neighbour about anything the seller has or has not done? If Yes, please give details:

☐ Yes   ☐ No

8.2 Has the seller complained or had cause to complain to or about the landlord, the management company, or any neighbour? If Yes, please give details:
☐ Yes   ☐ No

9 Alterations

9.1 Is the seller aware of any alterations having been made to the property since the lease was originally granted?
☐ Yes   ☐ No

If No, please go to section 10 'Enfranchisement' and do not answer 9.2 and 9.3 below.

9.2 Please give details of these alterations:

9.3 Was the landlord's consent for the alterations obtained? If Yes, please supply a copy.
☐ Yes   ☐ No
☐ Not known   ☐ Not required
☐ Enclosed   ☐ To follow

10 Enfranchisement

Note: 'enfranchisement' is the right of a tenant to purchase the freehold from their landlord and the right of the tenant to extend the term of the lease.

10.1 Has the seller owned the property for a least two years?
☐ Yes   ☐ No

10.2 Has the seller served on the landlord a formal notice stating the seller's wish to buy the freehold or be granted an extended lease? If Yes, please supply a copy.
☐ Yes   ☐ No
☐ Enclosed   ☐ To follow
☐ Lost

10.3 Is the seller aware of the service of any notice relating to the possible collective purchase of the freehold of the building or part of it by a group of tenants? If Yes, please supply a copy.
☐ Yes   ☐ No
☐ Enclosed   ☐ To follow
☐ Lost

10.4 Is the seller aware of any response to a notice disclosed in replies to 10.2 and 10.3 above? If Yes, please supply a copy.
☐ Yes   ☐ No
☐ Enclosed   ☐ To follow
☐ Lost

Signed: ....   Dated: ....

Each seller should sign this form.

The Law Society

The Law Society is the representative body for solicitors in England and Wales.   © Law Society 2009

TA8 New home information form[1]

---

[1] © Law Society 2007.

New home information form

Document date ☐ D ☐ D / ☐ M ☐ M / ☐ Y ☐ Y

Address or proposed address of the property

Postcode ☐☐☐☐☐☐☐   Plot number ☐

This form should be completed and read in conjunction with the explanatory notes available separately

1 For all properties

1. Please confirm that an Energy Performance Certificate will be provided as soon as the property is physically complete.   ☐ Yes

2. Please state the estimated dates for:

   (a) physical completion of the property

   (b) certification that the property is fit for occupation

3. Is the warranty of any professional consultant available in relation to the monitoring of the construction or conversion of the property?   ☐ Yes   ☐ No

   If Yes, please give details:

4. Are all easements necessary for the enjoyment of the property fully available?   ☐ Yes   ☐ No

   If No, please give details:

The Law Society

TA8

© Law Society 2007

5. Is there any road or sewer abutting or serving the property that has not been adopted?

   ☐ Yes   ☐ No   ☐ Enclosed   ☐ To follow

   If Yes, please give details and supply a copy of any adoption agreement and bond:

6. Please specify which of the following services are or will be connected to or at the property.

   If the supplies will be connected in the future, please also give the proposed dates of connection if known.

	Connected
Electricity	☐ Yes ☐ N/A ☐ Will be D D / M M / Y Y
Gas	☐ Yes ☐ N/A ☐ Will be D D / M M / Y Y
Mains water	☐ Yes ☐ N/A ☐ Will be D D / M M / Y Y
Private drains	☐ Yes ☐ N/A ☐ Will be D D / M M / Y Y
Private water	☐ Yes ☐ N/A ☐ Will be D D / M M / Y Y
Septic tank/Cesspit	☐ Yes ☐ N/A ☐ Will be D D / M M / Y Y
Telephone	☐ Yes ☐ N/A ☐ Will be D D / M M / Y Y

7. Which if any of the following services at the property are
fully operational?

Boiler	☐ Yes	☐ No	☐ N/A
Space heating	☐ Yes	☐ No	☐ N/A
Water heating	☐ Yes	☐ No	☐ N/A
Lift	☐ Yes	☐ No	☐ N/A

If No, for any of these services, please give details:

8. Please provide copies of any guarantees that are
available or will be available at completion in relation
to the following:

Damp	☐ Yes ☐ To follow	☐ No	☐ Enclosed
Double glazing, roof lights, roof windows, glazed doors	☐ Yes ☐ To follow	☐ No	☐ Enclosed
Electrical appliances	☐ Yes ☐ To follow	☐ No	☐ Enclosed
Electrical work	☐ Yes ☐ To follow	☐ No	☐ Enclosed
Heating systems	☐ Yes ☐ To follow	☐ No	☐ Enclosed
Hot water systems	☐ Yes ☐ To follow	☐ No	☐ Enclosed
New home warranty	☐ Yes ☐ To follow	☐ No	☐ Enclosed
Timber infestation	☐ Yes ☐ To follow	☐ No	☐ Enclosed
Roofing	☐ Yes ☐ To follow	☐ No	☐ Enclosed
Ventilation systems	☐ Yes ☐ To follow	☐ No	☐ Enclosed

APPENDIX B3

9. Has any application been made for street naming and numbering and for allocation of a postcode?

☐ Yes ☐ No ☐ Enclosed ☐ To follow

If Yes, please provide copies of responses.

10. Please confirm whether the property has:

(a) been inspected by the valuation officer ☐ Yes ☐ No

If No, please give details:

[ ]

or

(b) entered on the valuation list for council tax ☐ Yes ☐ No

If No, please give details:

[ ]

11. Please state the council tax valuation band for the property and the amount of the annual payment.

Band A - H [ ]

Amount £ [ ] yearly

12. Has the billing authority issued any completion notice in respect of the property? ☐ Yes ☐ No

If No, please give details:

[ ]

2 Leasehold

1. Please provide a copy of any budget or estimate for payments in the 12 months after completion in respect of service and maintenance charges, insurance and any reserve fund.

☐ Enclosed ☐ To follow

2. Have managing agents been appointed or is it intended that managing agents will be appointed?

☐ Yes ☐ No ☐ To be appointed

If Yes, or to be appointed, please give contact details including name, address, telephone number, and email:

[ ]

TA8 New home information form   www.lawsociety.org.uk

3. Has any management company been formed in respect
of which any shares are to be issued to the buyer or any
other occupier of a flat within the development?

☐ Yes ☐ No

If Yes, please give details:

4. Are there any communal or shared areas or other parts
of the development that will remain to be completed
after completion of the property?

☐ Yes ☐ No

If Yes, please give details:

5. Is there any contract or arrangement for the sale of the
freehold reversion?

☐ Yes ☐ No

If Yes, please give details:

6. Are any negotiations in progress for the sale of the
freehold reversion?

☐ Yes ☐ No

If Yes, please give details:

3 Commonhold

1. Please provide a copy of any budget or estimate for the
commonhold assessment payments in the 12 months
after completion in respect of maintenance charges,
insurance and any reserve fund.

☐ Enclosed ☐ To follow

2. Please provide the contact details of the
commonhold association:

3. Have managing agents been appointed or is it intended that managing agents will be appointed?

    ☐ Yes   ☐ No   ☐ To be appointed

    If Yes, or to be appointed, please give contact details including name, address, telephone number, and email:

4. How many unit holders will there be?

5. Are there any communal or shared areas or other parts of the development that will remain to be completed after completion of the property?

    ☐ Yes   ☐ No

    If Yes, please give details:

6. When will the transfer of the common parts take place?

    D D / M M / Y Y

7. Does the commonhold community statement give 'development rights'?

    ☐ Yes   ☐ No

    If Yes, please give details:

The information in this form has been given by:

Name

The Law Society

82

APPENDIX B4

TA9 Commonhold information form[1]

Commonhold information form

Document date [D][D] / [M][M] / [Y][Y]

Address of the property

Postcode [ ][ ][ ][ ][ ][ ][ ]

This form should be completed and read in conjunction with the explanatory notes available separately

1 Commonhold association

1.1 Please supply copies of the commonhold association's accounts for the last three years.

☐ Enclosed ☐ To follow ☐ Lost

1.2 Please supply the names and addresses of:

(a) the directors of the association

(b) the secretary of the association

(c) any managing agents appointed by the association

1.3 Does the seller know of any proposal to amend the terms of the commonhold community statement?

☐ Yes ☐ No

If Yes, please give details:

The Law Society

TA9

© Law Society 2007

1.4 Does the seller know of any proposal to enlarge the commonhold?   ☐ Yes   ☐ No

If Yes, please give details:

1.5 Is the commonhold association a member of an approved ombudsman scheme?   ☐ Yes   ☐ No

If Yes, please give the ombudsman's name and address:

2 Commonhold assessments and reserve fund levies

2.1 Has the commonhold association made any commonhold assessments in respect of the seller's unit during the last three years?   ☐ Yes   ☐ No

If Yes, please give details:

2.2 Has the commonhold association established any reserve funds (to pay for major expenditure on such items as outside painting, roof repairs, lift replacement)?   ☐ Yes   ☐ No

If Yes, please give details:

2.3 Has the commonhold association made levies (demanded contributions) in respect of the seller's unit during the last three years?   ☐ Yes   ☐ No

If Yes, please give details of how much was payable to which fund:

2.4 Does the seller know of any expense, which is not usually incurred every year and is not covered by a reserve fund (e.g. redecoration, repairing drives), which the commonhold association is likely to incur within the next three years?

☐ Yes   ☐ No

If Yes, please give details:

2.5 Has the seller challenged, or does the seller know of any other unit-holder who has challenged, the amount of any commonhold assessment or reserve fund levy during the last three years?

☐ Yes   ☐ No

If Yes, please give details:

2.6 Does the seller know of any problems in the last three years between unit-holders and the commonhold association about the payment of commonhold assessments or reserve fund levies?

☐ Yes   ☐ No

If Yes, please give details:

2.7 Please obtain a commonhold unit information certificate from the commonhold association and supply a copy.

☐ Enclosed   ☐ To follow

3 Notices

3.1 Has the seller had any notice about the unit being sold or any other part of the commonhold, its use, its condition, or its repair and maintenance?

☐ Yes   ☐ No   ☐ Enclosed
☐ To follow

If Yes, please supply a copy.

Note: A notice could be in a printed form or in the form of a letter. It could come from the commonhold association, another unit-holder, a neighbouring owner or an official body.

www.lawsociety.org.uk

Commonhold information form **TA9**

86

4 Common parts

4.1 Does the seller know of any dispute about the use of the common parts during the last three years?

☐ Yes ☐ No

If Yes, please give details:

4.2 Does the seller know of any proposal to lease or dispose of any of the common parts?

☐ Yes ☐ No

If Yes, please give details:

4.3 Does the seller know of any proposal to mortgage all or any part of the common parts?

☐ Yes ☐ No

If Yes, please give details:

5 Insurance

5.1 Please supply a copy of the insurance policy covering the unit being sold (whether or not the policy also covers other property) and evidence of payment of the latest premium. (If the commonhold association arranges the insurance, please obtain particulars from the association.)

☐ Enclosed ☐ To follow

5.2 If the common parts are separately insured, please obtain from the commonhold association, and supply a copy of, the insurance policy covering the common parts and evidence of payment of the latest premium.

☐ Enclosed ☐ To follow

TA9 *Commonhold information form*

www.lawsociety.org.uk

87

6 Consents

6.1 Does the seller know if the commonhold association has given its consent to the transfer of part only of any of the units?　　□ Yes　　□ No

If Yes, please give details:

6.2 Does the seller know if the commonhold association has refused to give its consent to the transfer of part only of any of the units?　　□ Yes　　□ No

If Yes, please give details:

7 Complaints

7.1 Has the seller received any complaint from the commonhold association, another unit-holder or the occupier of any unit about anything you have or have not done?　　□ Yes　　□ No

If Yes, please give details:

7.2 Has the seller complained to the commonhold association, another unit-holder or the occupier of any unit about anything they have or have not done?　　□ Yes　　□ No

If Yes, please give details:

7.3 Please supply a copy of any decision made by the ombudsman affecting the unit or the common parts.　　□ Enclosed　　□ To follow　　□ Not applicable

www.lawsociety.org.uk

Commonhold information form TA9

88

8 Rights for the developer

8.1 Has the developer ceased to be entitled to exercise any of the rights?

☐ Yes ☐ No ☐ Not applicable

If Yes, please give details including the name and address of the developer who is now entitled to exercise the rights:

Note: 'Development rights' may be rights to complete the building work, rights in connection with marketing units or the right to appoint directors of the commonhold association.

The information in this form has been given by:

Name

89

TA10 Fittings and contents form (third edition)[1]

Law Society Fittings and Contents Form (3rd edition)

Address of the property

Postcode ☐☐☐☐☐☐☐☐

Full names of the seller

Seller's solicitor

Name of solicitor's firm

Address

Email

Reference number

About this form

The aim of this form is to make clear to the buyer which items are included in the sale. It must be completed accurately by the seller as the form may become part of the contract between the buyer and seller.

It is important that sellers and buyers check the information in this form carefully.

Definitions

- 'Seller' means all sellers together where the property is owned by more than one person.
- 'Buyer' means all buyers together where the property is being bought by more than one person.

The Law Society

© Law Society 2013

91

Instructions to the seller and the buyer

In each row, the seller should tick the appropriate box to show whether:

- the item is included in the sale ('*Included*');
- the item is excluded from the sale ('*Excluded*');
- there is no such item at the property ('*None*').

Where an item is excluded from the sale the seller may offer it for sale by inserting a price in the appropriate box. The buyer can then decide whether to accept the seller's offer.

A seller who inserts a price in this form is responsible for negotiating the sale of that item directly with the buyer or through their estate agent. If the seller or buyer instructs their solicitor to negotiate the sale of such an item, there may be an additional charge.

Sellers and buyers should inform their solicitors of any arrangements made about items offered for sale.

If the seller removes any fixtures, fittings or contents, the seller should be reasonably careful to ensure that any damage caused is minimised.

Unless stated otherwise, the seller will be responsible for ensuring that all rubbish is removed from the property (including from the loft, garden, outbuildings, garages and sheds), and that the property is left in a reasonably clean and tidy condition.

1 Basic fittings

	Included	Excluded	None	Price	Comments
Boiler/immersion heater	☐	☐	☐		
Radiators/wall heaters	☐	☐	☐		
Night-storage heaters	☐	☐	☐		
Free-standing heaters	☐	☐	☐		
Gas fires (with surround)	☐	☐	☐		
Electric fires (with surround)	☐	☐	☐		
Light switches	☐	☐	☐		
Roof insulation	☐	☐	☐		
Window fittings	☐	☐	☐		
Window shutters/grilles	☐	☐	☐		
Internal door fittings	☐	☐	☐		
External door fittings	☐	☐	☐		
Doorbell/chime	☐	☐	☐		

1 Basic fittings (continued)

	Included	Excluded	None	Price	Comments
Electric sockets	☐	☐	☐	▭	
Burglar alarm	☐	☐	☐	▭	
Other items (please specify)					
	☐	☐		▭	
	☐	☐		▭	
	☐	☐		▭	
	☐	☐		▭	

2 Kitchen

Note: In this section please also indicate whether the item is fitted or freestanding.

	Fitted	Free-standing	Included	Excluded	None	Price	Comments
Hob	☐	☐	☐	☐	☐	▭	
Extractor hood	☐	☐	☐	☐	☐	▭	
Oven/grill	☐	☐	☐	☐	☐	▭	
Cooker	☐	☐	☐	☐	☐	▭	
Microwave	☐	☐	☐	☐	☐	▭	
Refrigerator/fridge-freezer	☐	☐	☐	☐	☐	▭	
Freezer	☐	☐	☐	☐	☐	▭	
Dishwasher	☐	☐	☐	☐	☐	▭	
Tumble-dryer	☐	☐	☐	☐	☐	▭	
Washing machine	☐	☐	☐	☐	☐	▭	
Other items (please specify)							
	☐	☐	☐	☐		▭	
	☐	☐	☐	☐		▭	
	☐	☐	☐	☐		▭	
	☐	☐	☐	☐		▭	

Law Society Fittings and Contents Form TA10

93

3 Bathroom

	Included	Excluded	None	Price	Comments
Bath	☐	☐	☐	☐	
Shower fitting for bath	☐	☐	☐	☐	
Shower curtain	☐	☐	☐	☐	
Bathroom cabinet	☐	☐	☐	☐	
Taps	☐	☐	☐	☐	
Separate shower and fittings	☐	☐	☐	☐	
Towel rail	☐	☐	☐	☐	
Soap/toothbrush holders	☐	☐	☐	☐	
Toilet roll holders	☐	☐	☐	☐	
Bathroom mirror	☐	☐	☐	☐	

4 Carpets

	Included	Excluded	None	Price	Comments
Hall, stairs and landing	☐	☐	☐	☐	
Living room	☐	☐	☐	☐	
Dining room	☐	☐	☐	☐	
Kitchen	☐	☐	☐	☐	
Bedroom 1	☐	☐	☐	☐	
Bedroom 2	☐	☐	☐	☐	
Bedroom 3	☐	☐	☐	☐	
Other rooms (please specify)					
	☐	☐		☐	
	☐	☐		☐	
	☐	☐		☐	
	☐	☐		☐	

5   Curtains and curtain rails

	Included	Excluded	None	Price	Comments
Curtain rails/poles/pelmets					
Hall, stairs and landing	☐	☐	☐	☐	
Living room	☐	☐	☐	☐	
Dining room	☐	☐	☐	☐	
Kitchen	☐	☐	☐	☐	
Bedroom 1	☐	☐	☐	☐	
Bedroom 2	☐	☐	☐	☐	
Bedroom 3	☐	☐	☐	☐	
Other rooms (please specify)					
	☐	☐		☐	
	☐	☐		☐	
	☐	☐		☐	
	☐	☐		☐	
Curtains/blinds					
Hall, stairs and landing	☐	☐	☐	☐	
Living room	☐	☐	☐	☐	
Dining room	☐	☐	☐	☐	
Kitchen	☐	☐	☐	☐	
Bedroom 1	☐	☐	☐	☐	
Bedroom 2	☐	☐	☐	☐	
Bedroom 3	☐	☐	☐	☐	
Other rooms (please specify)					
	☐	☐		☐	
	☐	☐		☐	
	☐	☐		☐	
	☐	☐		☐	

Law Society Fittings and Contents Form

6 Light fittings

Note: If the seller removes a light fitting, it is assumed that the seller will replace the fitting with a ceiling rose, a flex, bulb holder and bulb and that they will be left in a safe condition.

	Included	Excluded	None	Price	Comments
Hall, stairs and landing	☐	☐	☐	☐	
Living room	☐	☐	☐	☐	
Dining room	☐	☐	☐	☐	
Kitchen	☐	☐	☐	☐	
Bedroom 1	☐	☐	☐	☐	
Bedroom 2	☐	☐	☐	☐	
Bedroom 3	☐	☐	☐	☐	
Other rooms (please specify)					
	☐	☐		☐	
	☐	☐		☐	
	☐	☐		☐	
	☐	☐		☐	

7 Fitted units

Note: Fitted units include, for example, fitted cupboards, fitted shelves, and fitted wardrobes.

	Included	Excluded	None	Price	Comments
Hall, stairs and landing	☐	☐	☐	☐	
Living room	☐	☐	☐	☐	
Dining room	☐	☐	☐	☐	
Kitchen	☐	☐	☐	☐	
Bedroom 1	☐	☐	☐	☐	
Bedroom 2	☐	☐	☐	☐	
Bedroom 3	☐	☐	☐	☐	

7 Fitted units (continued)

	Included	Excluded	None	Price	Comments
Other rooms (please specify)					
	☐	☐		☐	
	☐	☐		☐	
	☐	☐		☐	
	☐	☐		☐	

8 Outdoor area

	Included	Excluded	None	Price	Comments
Garden furniture	☐	☐	☐	☐	
Garden ornaments	☐	☐	☐	☐	
Trees, plants, shrubs	☐	☐	☐	☐	
Barbecue	☐	☐	☐	☐	
Dustbins	☐	☐	☐	☐	
Garden shed	☐	☐	☐	☐	
Greenhouse	☐	☐	☐	☐	
Outdoor heater	☐	☐	☐	☐	
Outside lights	☐	☐	☐	☐	
Water butt	☐	☐	☐	☐	
Clothes line	☐	☐	☐	☐	
Rotary line	☐	☐	☐	☐	
Other items (please specify)					
	☐	☐		☐	
	☐	☐		☐	
	☐	☐		☐	
	☐	☐		☐	
	☐	☐		☐	

9 Television and telephone

	Included	Excluded	None	Price	Comments
Telephone receivers	☐	☐	☐	▭	
Television aerial	☐	☐	☐	▭	
Radio aerial	☐	☐	☐	▭	
Satellite dish	☐	☐	☐	▭	

10 Stock of fuel

	Included	Excluded	None	Price	Comments
Oil	☐	☐	☐	▭	
Wood	☐	☐	☐	▭	
Liquefied Petroleum Gas (LPG)	☐	☐	☐	▭	

11 Other items

	Included	Excluded	Price	Comments
	☐	☐	▭	
	☐	☐	▭	
	☐	☐	▭	
	☐	☐	▭	

Signed: .... Dated: ....

Signed: .... Dated: ....

Each seller should sign this form.

The Law Society is the representative body for solicitors in England and Wales.

TA13 Completion information and undertakings (third edition)[1]

---

[1] © Law Society . Third edition published 2019.

Completion information and undertakings (3rd edition)

WARNING: Replies to questions 3.2, 5.2 and 5.3 are solicitor's undertakings.

Address of the property

Postcode ☐☐☐☐☐☐☐

Seller

Buyer

---

1 Vacant possession

1.1 If vacant possession (of whole or part) is to be given on completion what arrangements will be made to hand over the keys?

☐ will be left with agents
☐ will be left with seller's solicitors
☐ other (please give details)

1.2 If vacant possession (of whole or part) is not being given, please confirm that an authority to the tenant to pay the rent to the buyer will be handed over or be included with the documents to be remitted to the buyer's solicitors on completion.

☐ Confirmed

The Law Society

www.lawsociety.org.uk

TA13

2 **Deeds and documents**

2.1 If the title is unregistered, do you hold all of the title deeds? ☐ Yes ☐ No

If No, please give details:

2.2 Please list all deeds and documents to be sent on completion.

-
-
-
-
-
-

3 **Completion**

3.1 Will completion take place at your office? ☐ Yes ☐ No

If No, where or how will it take place?

3.2 We wish to complete through the post in accordance with the Law Society's Code for Completion by Post 2019 (the Code). Please confirm that:

(a) You undertake to adopt the Code; and ☐ Confirmed

(b) The mortgages and charges that you undertake to redeem or discharge in your replies to 5.1 and 5.2 are those specified for the purpose of paragraph 7 of the Code. ☐ Confirmed

The Law Society

4 Money

WARNING: Be alert to the risks of emailing bank details.

4.1 Please state the exact amount payable on completion.

£ _____

If it is not just the balance purchase money, please provide copy receipts for any rent or service charge or other payments being apportioned.

☐ Enclosed ☐ Not applicable

4.2 Please provide details of your bank and the account to which completion monies are to be sent:

Name of bank
_____

Address of bank
_____

Branch sort code
☐☐ ☐☐ ☐☐

Client account name
_____

Client account number
_____

5 Mortgages and charges

5.1 Please list the mortgages or charges secured on the property which you undertake to redeem or discharge to the extent that they relate to the property on or before completion (this includes repayment of any discount under the Housing Acts).

_____

The Law Society

The Law Society is the representative body for solicitors in England and Wales.

© Law Society 2019

5.2 Do you undertake to redeem or discharge the mortgages and charges listed in reply to 5.1 on completion and to send to us Form DS1, DS3, the receipted charge(s) or confirmation that notice of release or discharge in electronic form has been given to HM Land Registry as and when you receive them?

☐ Yes ☐ No

5.3 If you **DO NOT** agree to adopt the current Law Society's Code for Completion by Post, please confirm that you are the duly authorised agent of the proprietor of every mortgage or charge on the property which you have undertaken, in reply to 5.2, to redeem or discharge.

☐ Confirmed

Buyer's solicitor

Seller's solicitor

Date ☐☐ / ☐☐ / ☐☐

Date ☐☐ / ☐☐ / ☐☐

The Law Society

The Law Society is the representative body for solicitors in England and Wales.

© Law Society 2019

APPENDIX C

Standard Conditions of Sale (fifth edition – 2018 revision) (including explanatory notes)[1]

CONTRACT
INCORPORATING THE STANDARD CONDITIONS OF SALE
(FIFTH EDITION – 2018 REVISION)

Date	:
Seller	:
Buyer	:
Property (freehold/leasehold)	:
Title number/root of title	:
Specified incumbrances	:
Title guarantee (full/limited)	:
Completion date	:
Contract rate	:
Purchase price	:
Deposit	:
Contents price (if separate)	:
Balance	:

The seller will sell and the buyer will buy the property for the purchase price.

---

[1]   © Oyez (The Solicitors' Law Stationery Society Ltd) and the Law Society 2011. Revised 2018.

WARNING	Signed
This is a formal document, designed to create legal rights and legal obligations. Take advice before using it.	
	Seller/Buyer

STANDARD CONDITIONS OF SALE (FIFTH EDITION – 2018 REVISION) (NATIONAL CONDITIONS OF SALE 25TH EDITION, LAW SOCIETY'S CONDITIONS OF SALE 2011)

1. GENERAL

1.1 Definitions

1.1.1   In these conditions:

    (a)   'accrued interest' means:

        (i)   if money has been placed on deposit or in a building society share account, the interest actually earned

        (ii)   otherwise, the interest which might reasonably have been earned by depositing the money at interest on seven days' notice of withdrawal with a clearing bank less, in either case, any proper charges for handling the money

    (b)   'clearing bank' means a bank admitted by the Bank of England as a direct participant in its CHAPS system

    (c)   'completion date' has the meaning given in condition 6.1.1

    (d)   'contents price' means any separate amount payable for contents included in the contract

    (e)   'contract rate' means the Law Society's interest rate from time to time in force

    (f)   'conveyancer' means a solicitor, barrister, duly certified notary public, licensed conveyancer or recognised body under sections 9 or 23 of the Administration of Justice Act 1985

    (g)   'lease' includes sub-lease, tenancy and agreement for a lease or sub-lease

    (h)   'mortgage' means a mortgage or charge securing the repayment of money

    (i)   'notice to complete' means a notice requiring completion of the contract in accordance with condition 6.8

    (j)   'public requirement' means any notice, order or proposal given or made (whether before or after the date of the contract) by a body acting on statutory authority

    (k)   'requisition' includes objection

    (l)   'transfer' includes conveyance and assignment

    (m)   'working day' means any day from Monday to Friday (inclusive) which is not Christmas Day, Good Friday or a statutory Bank Holiday.

1.1.2   In these conditions the terms 'absolute title' and 'official copies' have the special meanings given to them by the Land Registration Act 2002.

1.1.3   A party is ready, able and willing to complete:

    (a)   if he could be, but for the default of the other party, and

    (b)   in the case of the seller, even though the property remains subject to a mortgage, if

105

the amount to be paid on completion enables the property to be transferred freed of all mortgages (except any to which the sale is expressly subject).

1.1.4   These conditions apply except as varied or excluded by the contract.

1.2   Joint parties

If there is more than one seller or more than one buyer, the obligations which they undertake can be enforced against them all jointly or against each individually.

1.3   Notices and documents

1.3.1   A notice required or authorised by the contract must be in writing.

1.3.2   Giving a notice or delivering a document to a party's conveyancer has the same effect as giving or delivering it to that party.

1.3.3   Where delivery of the original document is not essential, a notice or document is validly given or sent if it is sent:
(a)   by fax, or
(b)   by e-mail to an e-mail address for the intended recipient given in the contract.

1.3.4   Subject to conditions 1.3.5 to 1.3.7, a notice is given and a document is delivered when it is received.

1.3.5 (a)   A notice or document sent through a document exchange is received when it is available for collection.
(b)   A notice or document which is received after 4.00 pm on a working day, or on a day which is not a working day, is to be treated as having been received on the next working day.
(c)   An automated response to a notice or document sent by e-mail that the intended recipient is out of the office is to be treated as proof that the notice or document was not received.

1.3.6   Condition 1.3.7 applies unless there is proof:
(a)   that a notice or document has not been received, or
(b)   of when it was received.

1.3.7   A notice or document sent by the following means is treated as having been received as follows:
(a)   by first-class post: before 4.00 pm on the second working day after posting
(b)   by second-class post: before 4.00 pm on the third working day after posting
(c)   through a document exchange: before 4.00 pm on the first working day after the day on which it would normally be available for collection by the addressee
(d)   by fax: one hour after despatch
(e)   by e-mail: before 4.00 pm on the first working day after despatch.

1.4   VAT

1.4.1   The purchase price and the contents price are inclusive of any value added tax.

1.4.2   All other sums made payable by the contract are exclusive of any value added tax and where a supply is made which is chargeable to value added tax, the recipient of the supply is to pay the supplier (in addition to any other amounts payable under the contract) a sum equal to the value added tax chargeable on that supply.

1.5 Assignment and sub-sales

1.5.1   The buyer is not entitled to transfer the benefit of the contract.

1.5.2   The seller cannot be required to transfer the property in parts or to any person other than the buyer.

1.6 Third party rights

Unless otherwise expressly stated nothing in this contract will create rights pursuant to the Contracts (Rights of Third Parties) Act 1999 in favour of anyone other than the parties to the contract.

2.   FORMATION

2.1 Date

2.1.1   If the parties intend to make a contract by exchanging duplicate copies by post or through a document exchange, the contract is made when the last copy is posted or deposited at the document exchange.

2.1.2   If the parties' conveyancers agree to treat exchange as taking place before duplicate copies are actually exchanged, the contract is made as so agreed.

2.2 Deposit

2.2.1   The buyer is to pay or send a deposit of 10 per cent of the purchase price no later than the date of the contract.

2.2.2   If a cheque tendered in payment of all or part of the deposit is dishonoured when first presented, the seller may, within seven working days of being notified that the cheque has been dishonoured, give notice to the buyer that the contract is discharged by the buyer's breach.

2.2.3   Conditions 2.2.4 to 2.2.6 do not apply on a sale by auction.

2.2.4   The deposit is to be paid:
- (a)   by electronic means from an account held in the name of a conveyancer at a clearing bank to an account in the name of the seller's conveyancer or (in a case where condition 2.2.5 applies) a conveyancer nominated by him and maintained at a clearing bank, or
- (b)   to the seller's conveyancer or (in a case where condition 2.2.5 applies) a conveyancer nominated by him by cheque drawn on a solicitor's or licensed conveyancer's client account.

2.2.5   If before completion date the seller agrees to buy another property in England and Wales for his residence, he may use all or any part of the deposit as a deposit in that transaction to be held on terms to the same effect as this condition and condition 2.2.6.

2.2.6   Any deposit or part of a deposit not being used in accordance with condition 2.2.5 is to be held by the seller's conveyancer as stakeholder on terms that on completion it is paid to the seller with accrued interest.

2.3   Auctions

2.3.1   On a sale by auction the following conditions apply to the property and, if it is sold in lots, to each lot.

2.3.2   The sale is subject to a reserve price.

2.3.3   The seller, or a person on his behalf, may bid up to the reserve price.

2.3.4   The auctioneer may refuse any bid.

2.3.5   If there is a dispute about a bid, the auctioneer may resolve the dispute or restart the auction at the last undisputed bid.

2.3.6   The deposit is to be paid to the auctioneer as agent for the seller.

3.   MATTERS AFFECTING THE PROPERTY

3.1   Freedom from incumbrances

3.1.1   The seller is selling the property free from incumbrances, other than those mentioned in condition 3.1.2.

3.1.2   The incumbrances subject to which the property is sold are:
    (a)   those specified in the contract
    (b)   those discoverable by inspection of the property before the date of the contract
    (c)   those the seller does not and could not reasonably know about
    (d)   those, other than mortgages, which the buyer knows about
    (e)   entries made before the date of the contract in any public register except those maintained by the Land Registry or its Land Charges Department or by Companies House
    (f)   public requirements.

3.1.3   After the contract is made, the seller is to give the buyer written details without delay of any new public requirement and of anything in writing which he learns about concerning a matter covered by condition 3.1.2.

3.1.4   The buyer is to bear the cost of complying with any outstanding public requirement and is to indemnify the seller against any liability resulting from a public requirement.

3.2   Physical state

3.2.1   The buyer accepts the property in the physical state it is in at the date of the contract unless the seller is building or converting it.

3.2.2   A leasehold property is sold subject to any subsisting breach of a condition or tenant's obligation relating to the physical state of the property which renders the lease liable to forfeiture.

3.2.3   A sub-lease is granted subject to any subsisting breach of a condition or tenant's obligation relating to the physical state of the property which renders the seller's own lease liable to forfeiture.

3.3   Leases affecting the property

3.3.1   The following provisions apply if any part of the property is sold subject to a lease.

3.3.2 (a)   The seller having provided the buyer with full details of each lease or copies of the documents embodying the lease terms, the buyer is treated as entering into the contract knowing and fully accepting those terms.

(b)   The seller is to inform the buyer without delay if the lease ends or if the seller learns of any application by the tenant in connection with the lease; the seller is then to act as the buyer reasonably directs, and the buyer is to indemnify him against all consequent loss and expense.

(c)   Except with the buyer's consent, the seller is not to agree to any proposal to change the lease terms nor to take any step to end the lease.

(d)   The seller is to inform the buyer without delay of any change to the lease terms which may be proposed or agreed.

(e)   The buyer is to indemnify the seller against all claims arising from the lease after actual completion; this includes claims which are unenforceable against a buyer for want of registration.

(f)   The seller takes no responsibility for what rent is lawfully recoverable, nor for whether or how any legislation affects the lease.

(g)   If the let land is not wholly within the property, the seller may apportion the rent.

4.   TITLE AND TRANSFER

4.1   Proof of title

4.1.1   Without cost to the buyer, the seller is to provide the buyer with proof of the title to the property and of his ability to transfer it, or to procure its transfer.

4.1.2   Where the property has a registered title the proof is to include official copies of the items referred to in rules 134(1)(a) and (b) and 135(1)(a) of the Land Registration Rules 2003, so far as they are not to be discharged or overridden at or before completion.

4.1.3   Where the property has an unregistered title, the proof is to include:

(a)   an abstract of title or an epitome of title with photocopies of the documents, and

(b)   production of every document or an abstract, epitome or copy of it with an original marking by a conveyancer either against the original or an examined abstract or an examined copy.

4.2   Requisitions

4.2.1   The buyer may not raise requisitions:

(a)   on any title shown by the seller before the contract was made

(b)   in relation to the matters covered by condition 3.1.2.

4.2.2   Notwithstanding condition 4.2.1, the buyer may, within six working days of a matter coming to his attention after the contract was made, raise written requisitions on that matter. In that event, steps 3 and 4 in condition 4.3.1 apply.

4.2.3   On the expiry of the relevant time limit under condition 4.2.2 or condition 4.3.1, the buyer loses his right to raise requisitions or to make observations.

4.3   Timetable

4.3.1   Subject to condition 4.2 and to the extent that the seller did not take the steps described in condition 4.1.1 before the contract was made, the following are the steps for deducing and investigating the title to the property to be taken within the following time limits:

Step		Time Limit
1.	The seller is to comply with condition 4.1.1	Immediately after making the contract
2.	The buyer may raise written requisitions	Six working days after either the date of the contract or the date of delivery of the seller's evidence of title on which the requisitions are raised whichever is the later
3.	The seller is to reply in writing to any requisitions raised	Four working days after receiving the requisitions
4.	The buyer may make written observations on the seller's replies	Three working days after receiving the replies

The time limit on the buyer's right to raise requisitions applies even where the seller supplies incomplete evidence of his title, but the buyer may, within six working days from delivery of any further evidence, raise further requisitions resulting from that evidence.

4.3.2   The parties are to take the following steps to prepare and agree the transfer of the property within the following time limits:

Step		Time Limit
A.	The buyer is to send the seller a draft transfer	At least twelve working days before completion date
B.	The seller is to approve or revise that draft and either return it or retain it for use as the actual transfer	Four working days after delivery of the draft transfer
C.	If the draft is returned the buyer is to send an engrossment to the seller	At least five working days before completion date

4.3.3   Periods of time under conditions 4.3.1 and 4.3.2 may run concurrently.

4.3.4   If the period between the date of the contract and completion date is less than 15 working days, the time limits in conditions 4.2.2, 4.3.1 and 4.3.2 are to be reduced by the same proportion as that period bears to the period of 15 working days. Fractions of a working day are to be rounded down except that the time limit to perform any step is not to be less than one working day.

4.4   Defining the property

The seller need not:
    (a)   prove the exact boundaries of the property

(b)   prove who owns fences, ditches, hedges or walls

(c)   separately identify parts of the property with different titles further than he may be able to do from information in his possession.

4.5   Rents and rentcharges

The fact that a rent or rentcharge, whether payable or receivable by the owner of the property, has been, or will on completion be, informally apportioned is not to be regarded as a defect in title.

4.6   Transfer

4.6.1   The buyer does not prejudice his right to raise requisitions, or to require replies to any raised, by taking any steps in relation to preparing or agreeing the transfer.

4.6.2   Subject to condition 4.6.3, the seller is to transfer the property with full title guarantee.

4.6.3   The transfer is to have effect as if the disposition is expressly made subject to all matters covered by condition 3.1.2 and, if the property is leasehold, is to contain a statement that the covenants set out in section 4 of the Law of Property (Miscellaneous Provisions) Act 1994 will not extend to any breach of the tenant's covenants in the lease relating to the physical state of the property.

4.6.4   If after completion the seller will remain bound by any obligation affecting the property which was disclosed to the buyer before the contract was made, but the law does not imply any covenant by the buyer to indemnify the seller against liability for future breaches of it:

(a)   the buyer is to covenant in the transfer to indemnify the seller against liability for any future breach of the obligation and to perform it from then on, and

(b)   if required by the seller, the buyer is to execute and deliver to the seller on completion a duplicate transfer prepared by the buyer.

4.6.5   The seller is to arrange at his expense that, in relation to every document of title which the buyer does not receive on completion, the buyer is to have the benefit of:

(a)   a written acknowledgement of his right to its production, and

(b)   a written undertaking for its safe custody (except while it is held by a mortgagee or by someone in a fiduciary capacity).

4.7   Membership of company

Where the seller is, or is required to be, a member of a company that has an interest in the property or has management responsibilities for the property or the surrounding areas, the seller is, without cost to the buyer, to provide such documents on completion as will enable the buyer to become a member of that company.

5.   RISK, INSURANCE AND OCCUPATION PENDING COMPLETION

5.1.1   The property is at the risk of the buyer from the date of the contract.

5.1.2   The seller is under no obligation to the buyer to insure the property unless:

(a) the contract provides that a policy effected by or for the seller and insuring the property or any part of it against liability for loss or damage is to continue in force, or

(b) the property or any part of it is let on terms under which the seller (whether as landlord or as tenant) is obliged to insure against loss or damage.

5.1.3 If the seller is obliged to insure the property under condition 5.1.2, the seller is to:
(a) do everything necessary to maintain the policy
(b) permit the buyer to inspect the policy or evidence of its terms
(c) if before completion the property suffers loss or damage:

(i) pay to the buyer on completion the amount of the policy monies which the seller has received, so far as not applied in repairing or reinstating the property, and

(ii) if no final payment has then been received, assign to the buyer, at the buyer's expense, all rights to claim under the policy in such form as the buyer reasonably requires and pending execution of the assignment hold any policy monies received in trust for the buyer

(d) cancel the policy on completion.

5.1.4 Where the property is leasehold and the property, or any building containing it, is insured by a reversioner or other third party, the seller is to use reasonable efforts to ensure that the insurance is maintained until completion and if, before completion, the property or building suffers loss or damage the seller is to assign to the buyer on completion, at the buyer's expense, such rights as the seller may have in the policy monies, in such form as the buyer reasonably requires.

5.1.5 If payment under a policy effected by or for the buyer is reduced, because the property is covered against loss or damage by an insurance policy effected by or on behalf of the seller, then, unless the seller is obliged to insure the property under condition 5.1.2, the purchase price is to be abated by the amount of that reduction.

5.1.6 Section 47 of the Law of Property Act 1925 does not apply.

5.2 Occupation by buyer

5.2.1 If the buyer is not already lawfully in the property, and the seller agrees to let him into occupation, the buyer occupies on the following terms.

5.2.2 The buyer is a licensee and not a tenant. The terms of the licence are that the buyer:
(a) cannot transfer it
(b) may permit members of his household to occupy the property
(c) is to pay or indemnify the seller against all outgoings and other expenses in respect of the property
(d) is to pay the seller a fee calculated at the contract rate on a sum equal to the purchase price (less any deposit paid) for the period of the licence
(e) is entitled to any rents and profits from any part of the property which he does not occupy
(f) is to keep the property in as good a state of repair as it was in when he went into occupation (except for fair wear and tear) and is not to alter it
(g) if the property is leasehold, is not to do anything which puts the seller in breach of his obligations in the lease, and
(h) is to quit the property when the licence ends.

5.2.3   The buyer is not in occupation for the purposes of this condition if he merely exercises rights of access given solely to do work agreed by the seller.

5.2.4   The buyer's licence ends on the earliest of: completion date, rescission of the contract or when five working days' notice given by one party to the other takes effect.

5.2.5   If the buyer is in occupation of the property after his licence has come to an end and the contract is subsequently completed he is to pay the seller compensation for his continued occupation calculated at the same rate as the fee mentioned in condition 5.2.2(d).

5.2.6   The buyer's right to raise requisitions is unaffected.

6. COMPLETION

6.1   Date

6.1.1   Completion date is twenty working days after the date of the contract but time is not of the essence of the contract unless a notice to complete has been served.

6.1.2   If the money due on completion is received after 2.00 pm, completion is to be treated, for the purposes only of conditions 6.3 and 7.2, as taking place on the next working day as a result of the buyer's default.

6.1.3   Condition 6.1.2 does not apply and the seller is treated as in default if:
    (a)   the sale is with vacant possession of the property or any part of it, and
    (b)   the buyer is ready, able and willing to complete but does not pay the money due on completion until after 2.00 pm because the seller has not vacated the property or that part by that time.

6.2   Arrangements and place

6.2.1   The buyer's conveyancer and the seller's conveyancer are to co-operate in agreeing arrangements for completing the contract.

6.2.2   Completion is to take place in England and Wales, either at the seller's conveyancer's office or at some other place which the seller reasonably specifies.

6.3   Apportionments

6.3.1   On evidence of proper payment being made, income and outgoings of the property are to be apportioned between the parties so far as the change of ownership on completion will affect entitlement to receive or liability to pay them.

6.3.2   If the whole property is sold with vacant possession or the seller exercises his option in condition 7.2.4, apportionment is to be made with effect from the date of actual completion; otherwise, it is to be made from completion date.

6.3.3   In apportioning any sum, it is to be assumed that the seller owns the property until the end of the day from which apportionment is made and that the sum accrues from day to day at the rate at which it is payable on that day.

6.3.4   For the purpose of apportioning income and outgoings, it is to be assumed that they accrue at an equal daily rate throughout the year.

6.3.5   When a sum to be apportioned is not known or easily ascertainable at completion, a provisional apportionment is to be made according to the best estimate available. As soon as the amount is known, a final apportionment is to be made and notified to the other party. Any resulting balance is to be paid no more than ten working days later, and if not then paid the balance is to bear interest at the contract rate from then until payment.

6.3.6   Compensation payable under condition 5.2.5 is not to be apportioned.

6.4   Amount payable

The amount payable by the buyer on completion is the purchase price and the contents price (less any deposit already paid to the seller or his agent) adjusted to take account of:
   (a)   apportionments made under condition 6.3
   (b)   any compensation to be paid or allowed under condition 7.2
   (c)   any sum payable under condition 5.1.3.

6.5   Title deeds

6.5.1   As soon as the buyer has complied with all his obligations under this contract on completion the seller must hand over the documents of title.

6.5.2   Condition 6.5.1 does not apply to any documents of title relating to land being retained by the seller after completion.

6.6   Rent receipts

The buyer is to assume that whoever gave any receipt for a payment of rent or service charge which the seller produces was the person or the agent of the person then entitled to that rent or service charge.

6.7   Means of payment

The buyer is to pay the money due on completion by a direct transfer of cleared funds from an account held in the name of a conveyancer at a clearing bank and, if appropriate, an unconditional release of a deposit held by a stakeholder.

6.8   Notice to complete

6.8.1   At any time after the time applicable under condition 6.1.2 on completion date, a party who is ready, able and willing to complete may give the other a notice to complete.

6.8.2   The parties are to complete the contract within ten working days of giving a notice to complete, excluding the day on which the notice is given. For this purpose, time is of the essence of the contract.

6.8.3   On receipt of a notice to complete:
   (a)   if the buyer paid no deposit, he is forthwith to pay a deposit of 10 per cent
   (b)   if the buyer paid a deposit of less than 10 per cent, he is forthwith to pay a further deposit equal to the balance of that 10 per cent.

7. REMEDIES

7.1 Errors and omissions

7.1.1   If any plan or statement in the contract, or in the negotiations leading to it, is or was misleading or inaccurate due to an error or omission by the seller, the remedies available to the buyer are as follows.

(a)   When there is a material difference between the description or value of the property, or of any of the contents included in the contract, as represented and as it is, the buyer is entitled to damages.

(b)   An error or omission only entitles the buyer to rescind the contract:

(i)   where it results from fraud or recklessness, or

(ii)   where he would be obliged, to his prejudice, to accept property differing substantially (in quantity, quality or tenure) from what the error or omission had led him to expect.

7.1.2   If either party rescinds the contract:

(a)   unless the rescission is a result of the buyer's breach of contract the deposit is to be repaid to the buyer with accrued interest

(b)   the buyer is to return any documents he received from the seller and is to cancel any registration of the contract.

7.2 Late completion

7.2.1   If there is default by either or both of the parties in performing their obligations under the contract and completion is delayed, the party whose total period of default is the greater is to pay compensation to the other party.

7.2.2   Compensation is calculated at the contract rate on an amount equal to the purchase price, less (where the buyer is the paying party) any deposit paid, for the period by which the paying party's default exceeds that of the receiving party, or, if shorter, the period between completion date and actual completion.

7.2.3   Any claim for loss resulting from delayed completion is to be reduced by any compensation paid under this contract.

7.2.4   Where the buyer holds the property as tenant of the seller and completion is delayed, the seller may give notice to the buyer, before the date of actual completion, that he intends to take the net income from the property until completion. If he does so, he cannot claim compensation under condition 7.2.1 as well.

7.3 After completion

Completion does not cancel liability to perform any outstanding obligation under this contract.

7.4 Buyer's failure to comply with notice to complete

7.4.1   If the buyer fails to complete in accordance with a notice to complete, the following terms apply.

7.4.2   The seller may rescind the contract, and if he does so:

115

(a)   he may:

    (i)   forfeit and keep any deposit and accrued interest
    (ii)   resell the property and any contents included in the contract
    (iii) claim damages

(b)   the buyer is to return any documents he received from the seller and is to cancel any registration of the contract.

7.4.3   The seller retains his other rights and remedies.

7.5   Seller's failure to comply with notice to complete

7.5.1   If the seller fails to complete in accordance with a notice to complete, the following terms apply.

7.5.2   The buyer may rescind the contract, and if he does so:
(a)   the deposit is to be repaid to the buyer with accrued interest
(b)   the buyer is to return any documents he received from the seller and is, at the seller's expense, to cancel any registration of the contract.

7.5.3   The buyer retains his other rights and remedies.

8.   LEASEHOLD PROPERTY

8.1   Existing leases

8.1.1   The following provisions apply to a sale of leasehold land.

8.1.2   The seller having provided the buyer with copies of the documents embodying the lease terms, the buyer is treated as entering into the contract knowing and fully accepting those terms.

8.2   New leases

8.2.1   The following provisions apply to a contract to grant a new lease.

8.2.2   The conditions apply so that:

    'seller' means the proposed landlord
    'buyer' means the proposed tenant
    'purchase price' means the premium to be paid on the grant of a lease.

8.2.3   The lease is to be in the form of the draft attached to the contract.

8.2.4   If the term of the new lease will exceed seven years, the seller is to deduce a title which will enable the buyer to register the lease at the Land Registry with an absolute title.

8.2.5   The seller is to engross the lease and a counterpart of it and is to send the counterpart to the buyer at least five working days before completion date.

8.2.6   The buyer is to execute the counterpart and deliver it to the seller on completion.

8.3   Consent

8.3.1 (a)   The following provisions apply if a consent to let, assign or sub-let is required to complete the contract.

(b)   In this condition 'consent' means consent in the form which satisfies the requirement to obtain it.

8.3.2 (a)   The seller is to apply for the consent at his expense, and to use all reasonable efforts to obtain it.

(b)   The buyer is to provide all information and references reasonably required.

8.3.3   Unless he is in breach of his obligation under condition 8.3.2, either party may rescind the contract by notice to the other party if three working days before completion date (or before a later date on which the parties have agreed to complete the contract):

(a)   the consent has not been given, or

(b)   the consent has been given subject to a condition to which a party reasonably objects. In that case, neither party is to be treated as in breach of contract and condition 7.1.2 applies.

9.   CONTENTS

9.1   The following provisions apply to any contents which are included in the contract, whether or not a separate price is to be paid for them.

9.2   The contract takes effect as a contract for sale of goods.

9.3   The buyer takes the contents in the physical state they are in at the date of the contract.

9.4   Ownership of the contents passes to the buyer on actual completion.

SPECIAL CONDITIONS

1   (a)   This contract incorporates the Standard Conditions of Sale (Fifth Edition).

(b)   The terms used in this contract have the same meaning when used in the Conditions.

2   Subject to the terms of this contract and to the Standard Conditions of Sale, the seller is to transfer the property with either full title guarantee or limited title guarantee, as specified on the front page.

3   (a)   The sale includes those contents which are indicated on the attached list as included in the sale and the buyer is to pay the contents price for them.

(b)   The sale excludes those fixtures which are at the property and are indicated on the attached list as excluded from the sale.

4   The property is sold with vacant possession.

(or)

4   The property is sold subject to the following leases or tenancies:

5   Conditions 6.1.2 and 6.1.3 shall take effect as if the time specified in them were [_____] rather than 2.00 pm.

6 Representations

Neither party can rely on any representation made by the other, unless made in writing by the other or his conveyancer, but this does not exclude liability for fraud or recklessness.

7 Occupier's consent

Each occupier identified below agrees with the seller and the buyer, in consideration of their entering into this contract, that the occupier concurs in the sale of the property on the terms of this contract, undertakes to vacate the property on or before the completion date and releases the property and any included fixtures and contents from any right or interest that the occupier may have.

Note: this condition does not apply to occupiers under leases or tenancies subject to which the property is sold

Name(s) and signature(s) of the occupier(s) (if any):

Name..

Signature..

Notices may be sent to:

Seller's conveyancer's name:
  E-mail address:*

Buyer's conveyancer's name:
  E-mail address:*

*Adding an e-mail address authorises service by e-mail: see condition 1.3.3(b).

EXPLANATORY NOTES ON THE STANDARD CONDITIONS OF SALE (FIFTH EDITION) (APRIL 2011)

GENERAL

The fifth edition of the Standard Conditions of Sale (the 'SCS') takes effect on 1 April 2011 and supersedes the fourth edition of the SCS issued in October 2003.

The revisions to the fourth edition have been made to bring the SCS in line with current law and practice with the aim of reducing the need for special conditions. The changes are intended to achieve a balance between the interests of the buyer and seller.

The main change is that, reflecting the position under the general law, the buyer is now to assume the risk from the date of exchange. Nonetheless, as explained below, there are certain cases in which the seller is obliged to insure.

The SCS are intended primarily for use in residential sales. Although they may be suitable for the sale of small business premises, conveyancers are likely to find that, for most commercial transactions, the Standard Commercial Property Conditions (the 'SCPC') are better suited to their needs.

The revisions maintain the policy of using plain English rather than legal terminology where possible.

The fifth edition of the SCS represents the 25th edition of the National Conditions of Sale and the Law Society's Conditions of Sale 2011.

DEFINITIONS

'contents price'

Condition 1.1.1(d) now refers to 'contents' rather than 'chattels'.

'direct credit'

The previous definition of 'direct credit' (meaning a 'direct transfer of cleared funds to an account nominated by the seller's conveyancer and maintained by a clearing bank') has been deleted, since this concept is now used only in condition 6.7. See also the explanation of the changes to condition 2.2.4.

'mortgage'

A new definition of 'mortgage' has been added, which clarifies the meaning of the term in condition 1.1.3(b) and is used in the new paragraph (d) of condition 3.1.2.

VAT

Condition 1.4.1 has been amended to make it clear that the agreed purchase price and contents price for a property are inclusive of VAT. This reflects the fact that the SCS are intended primarily to be used for residential transactions, which are usually exempt for VAT purposes.

If the sale does constitute a chargeable supply for VAT purposes, a special condition should be inserted if the seller requires the buyer to pay a sum equal to the VAT. In commercial or mixed use transactions, it is likely to be more appropriate to use the SCPC.

By virtue of condition 1.4.2, any other sums payable under the contract (i.e. sums other than the purchase price and contents price) will continue to be exclusive of VAT. In these circumstances, the recipient of a taxable supply will be liable to pay to the supplier a sum equal to the VAT chargeable on that supply.

ASSIGNMENT AND SUB-SALES

A new condition 1.5.2 provides that the seller cannot be required to transfer the property, or any part of it, to any person other than the buyer. The amendment is intended to protect the seller from becoming involved in a transaction with an unknown third party. This change clarifies the position and ensures consistency with the SCPC.

THIRD PARTY RIGHTS

Condition 1.6 has been added to exclude the operation of the Contracts (Rights of Third Parties) Act 1999. This ensures that a third party will not have any rights under the contract by virtue of that Act.

DEPOSIT

Condition 2.2.1 has been amended so that the 10% deposit is calculated by reference only to the purchase price and not, as before, the total of the purchase price and any separate contents price. This has been changed in order to provide certainty at an early stage as to the amount of the deposit that will be required. The buyer will not be required to pay 10% of the contents price, which can still be the subject of negotiation up until the point at which contracts are exchanged. If the deposit is also to take account of the contents price, this should be provided for by special condition. This change largely reflects practice.

As noted above, the definition of 'direct credit' has been deleted from the SCS. In condition 2.2.4, reference to 'direct credit' has been replaced by a reference to the deposit being paid by 'electronic means'. This has the effect that, unlike payments due on completion, the deposit does not have to be paid in cleared funds. Additional wording has been inserted so that the money transfer must now be made from an account held in the name of a conveyancer at a clearing bank to an account maintained at a clearing bank held in the name of either the seller's conveyancer or, where condition 2.2.5 applies, a conveyancer higher up the chain. It is hoped that limiting payments to those from a conveyancer's account will assist the seller's conveyancer in complying with anti-money laundering obligations. Express provision by way of special condition will be required for any alternative arrangements. Condition 2.2.4(b) continues to make provision for the payment of the deposit by cheque but, where condition 2.2.5 applies, now permits the cheque to be made payable to a conveyancer higher up the chain.

MATTERS AFFECTING THE PROPERTY

Condition 3.1.2(d) has been added to provide that the property is sold subject to any incumbrances (other than mortgages) which the buyer knows about. It is not considered fair for a buyer to be able to take action against a seller in respect of a matter which he knew about, but which was not expressly a matter subject to which the property was sold.

RETAINED LAND

Condition 3.4 in the fourth edition of the SCS has been deleted. It sought to deal with the situation where land is retained by the seller. Issues relating to retained land, such as rights and covenants, should be dealt with by way of special condition and by annexing an agreed form of transfer.

REQUISITIONS

The wording of condition 4.2.1(a) has been slightly amended to make it clear that the buyer cannot raise requisitions on any title shown by the seller before the contract was made. This is consistent with practice where title is deduced in full before exchange.

DEFINING THE PROPERTY

Condition 4.4.2 of the fourth edition has been deleted so that the buyer can no longer require the seller to provide a statutory declaration about facts relevant to matters such as boundaries, hedges, ditches and walls. It is not considered to be reasonable to expect the seller to provide a statutory declaration after exchange of contracts when investigation of title has taken place prior to exchange.

If necessary, this issue should be dealt with by special condition.

TRANSFER

The wording in condition 4.6.3 has been amended. In the case of a transfer of leasehold property, the contract requires the transfer to contain an express statement modifying the title guarantee by excluding the operation of section 4 of the Law of Property (Miscellaneous Provisions) Act 1994 in respect of any breach of the tenant's covenants in the lease relating to the physical state of the property. This has been inserted because similar provisions are widely used in practice and it is consistent with condition 3.2.2.

MEMBERSHIP OF COMPANY

Condition 4.7 has been inserted to enable the buyer to become a member of a management company or any other relevant company that has an interest in the property. This addition will reduce the need for a special condition to deal with this point. The condition stipulates that all relevant documents (which may include membership or share certificates and/or a duly signed stock transfer form) are to be provided to the buyer on completion. The condition has been drafted to apply not only to those companies with responsibilities in relation to leasehold property but also to those which have management obligations in relation to freehold property.

RISK, INSURANCE AND OCCUPATION PENDING COMPLETION

Significant changes have been made to the conditions relating to risk and insurance. The principal effect is that the risk position is reversed (from that in the fourth edition of the SCS) and the buyer bears the risk from exchange. Previous editions of the SCS left the risk with the seller until completion and, in practice, special conditions were frequently included to make the buyer bear the risk from exchange. This change brings the SCS broadly into line with the SCPC.

Even though the buyer takes the risk from exchange (meaning he still has to complete if the property is destroyed between exchange and completion), the seller may still have an obligation to insure the property between exchange and completion by virtue of condition 5.1.2. Under this condition, the seller is obliged to insure if the contract so provides or if the property is leasehold and the seller (whether as landlord or as tenant) is obliged to insure under the terms of the lease.

Condition 5.1.3 sets out the seller's obligations where he is required to insure.

Under condition 5.1.4, where the property is leasehold and insurance is effected by a landlord or other third party, the seller is to use reasonable efforts to ensure that the insurance is maintained until completion and if, before completion, the building suffers any loss or damage, the seller is to assign to the buyer any rights that the seller may have in the policy monies.

Condition 5.1.5 has been added in an attempt to clarify the position as regards 'double insurance'. This is where both the seller and buyer insure the property between exchange and completion. The new condition provides that where a payment under the buyer's insurance is reduced because the property is covered under an insurance policy taken out by or on behalf of the seller, then, provided the seller is not obliged to insure the property under condition 5.1.2, the purchase price is to be abated by the amount of that reduction. The position in this respect is now similar to that under the SCPC.

OCCUPATION BY BUYER

Condition 5.2.2(d) has been amended in line with condition 2.2.1 so that the licence fee is to be calculated by reference to the purchase price only.

Condition 5.2.2(g) of the fourth edition of the SCS, which dealt with the buyer's duty to insure the property, has been deleted because the risk will have passed to the buyer under the amended condition 5.1. The new condition 5.2.2(g) stipulates that, if the property is leasehold, the buyer is not to do anything which puts the seller in breach of his obligations in the lease.

APPORTIONMENTS

Condition 6.3.1 has been amended to require the party requesting apportionment to provide evidence of payment in relation to the relevant income and outgoings of the property.

TITLE DEEDS

The wording in condition 6.5.1 has been slightly amended so that the reference to the buyer's obligations is expressly limited to those under the SCS.

MEANS OF PAYMENT

The wording in condition 6.7 has been amended and now refers to a 'direct transfer' of cleared funds on completion. The previous edition used the defined term 'direct credit' which, as noted above, has been deleted in these conditions. This new wording makes it clear that the completion monies should come from and be paid to an account held in the name of a conveyancer. As with conditions 1.5.2 and 2.2.4, this change was made with the aim of combating fraud and assisting compliance with anti-money laundering measures.

NOTICE TO COMPLETE

Condition 6.8.1 has been amended so that notice to complete cannot be given before 2 pm on the day of completion. This change is intended to prevent the seller from serving a notice to complete on the morning of completion date.

LATE COMPLETION

Under condition 7.2.2, and in line with other relevant provisions in the SCS, compensation for late completion is calculated by reference to the purchase price only and not the purchase price and the contents price.

COMMONHOLD LAND

Condition 9 of the fourth edition of the SCS has been deleted. Commonhold is not widely used as a form of tenure. Where relevant, provision for commonhold land should be made by special condition.

CONTENTS

As previously noted, all references to 'chattels' in the SCS have been changed to 'contents'.

FRONT AND BACK PAGES

The general layout of the front page has been changed to allow conveyancers to record on the contract cover sheet details of the exchange of contracts including the names of the respective solicitors acting for the parties, the time of exchange and the relevant formula used.

SPECIAL CONDITIONS

Contents and fixtures

A revised special condition 3 makes clear which contents are included in the sale and which fixtures are excluded.

Completion

Special condition 5 allows the parties to vary condition 6.1.2 by specifying a time other than 2.00 pm in order to identify the day on which completion is to be treated as taking place for the purposes of condition 6.3 (apportionments) and 7.2 (compensation for late completion). This time will also become the earliest time for giving a notice to complete under condition 6.8.1. It is a special condition so that the parties will need to make a conscious decision if they wish to depart from the fallback provision in condition 6.1.2. It may be particularly useful where there is a chain of transactions. For example, the seller under the first contract in a chain might require payment of the purchase price by 1.30 pm to allow sufficient time to receive those funds and transmit them on his own purchase by 2.00 pm.

Representations

The limitation on liability for representations in special condition 6 aims to exclude liability for oral statements made by or on behalf of the parties. It does not exclude liability for fraud or recklessness. The exclusion is mutual but it is most likely in practice to be relied upon by the seller. Terms similar in effect to special condition 6 are commonly found in contracts. It has been included as a special condition (rather than one of the general conditions) in the light of judicial comments in *Morgan* v. *Pooley* [2010] EWHC 2447 (QB) that the clause in that case should be given effect because it was a special condition printed in large type and easily readable.

Occupier's consent

Special condition 7 is frequently required and has been inserted for ease of use and reference.

E-mail service of notice

The general position under the conditions is that service by e-mail is not authorised. If the parties wish to authorise service by e-mail they will need to add an e-mail address in the space indicated at the end of the special conditions.

The Law Society's formulae for exchanging contracts by telephone, fax or telex[1]

Introduction

It is essential that an agreed memorandum of the details and of any variations of the formula used should be made at the time and retained in the file. This would be very important if any question on the exchange were raised subsequently. Agreed variations should also be confirmed in writing. The serious risks of exchanging contracts without a deposit, unless the full implications are explained to and accepted by the seller client, are demonstrated in *Morris* v. *Duke-Cohan & Co.* (1975) 119 SJ 826.

As those persons involved in the exchange will bind their firms to the undertakings in the formula used, solicitors should carefully consider who is to be authorised to exchange contracts by telephone or telex and should ensure that the use of the procedure is restricted to them. Since professional undertakings form the basis of the formulae, they are only recommended for use between firms of solicitors and licensed conveyancers.

Law Society telephone/telex exchange – Formula A (1986)

(for use where one solicitor holds both signed parts of the contract):

A completion date of […] is agreed. The solicitor holding both parts of the contract confirms that he or she holds the part signed by his or her client(s), which is identical to the part he or she is also holding signed by the other solicitor's client(s) and will forthwith insert the agreed completion date in each part.

Solicitors mutually agree that exchange shall take place from that moment and the solicitor holding both parts confirms that, as of that moment, he or she holds the part signed by his or her client(s) to the order of the other. He or she undertakes that day by first class post, or where the other solicitor is a member of a document exchange (as to which the inclusion of a reference thereto in the solicitor's letterhead shall be conclusive evidence) by delivery to that or any other affiliated exchange, or by hand delivery direct to that solicitor's office, to send his or her signed part of the contract to the other solicitor, together, where he or she is the purchaser's solicitor, with a banker's draft or a solicitor's client account cheque for the deposit amounting to £.... .

---

[1] © The Law Society. Formulae A and B: 9 July 1986, revised January 1996. Formula C: 15 March 1989, revised January 1996. The formulae were previously published in *The Guide to the Professional Conduct of Solicitors 1999* as Annex 25D.

Note:

1.   *A memorandum should be prepared, after use of the formula, recording:*

   (a)   date and time of exchange;
   (b)   the formula used and exact wording of agreed variations;
   (c)   the completion date;
   (d)   the (balance) deposit to be paid;
   (e)   the identities of those involved in any conversation.

Law Society telephone/telex exchange – Formula B (1986)

(for use where each solicitor holds his or her own client's signed part of the contract):
   A completion date of [...] is agreed. Each solicitor confirms to the other that he or she holds a part contract in the agreed form signed by the client(s) and will forthwith insert the agreed completion date.
   Each solicitor undertakes to the other thenceforth to hold the signed part of the contract to the other's order, so that contracts are exchanged at that moment. Each solicitor further undertakes that day by first class post, or, where the other solicitor is a member of a document exchange (as to which the inclusion of a reference thereto in the solicitor's letterhead shall be conclusive evidence) by delivery to that or any other affiliated exchange, or by hand delivery direct to that solicitor's office, to send his or her signed part of the contract to the other together, in the case of a purchaser's solicitor, with a banker's draft or a solicitor's client account cheque for the deposit amounting to £....

Notes:

1.   *A memorandum should be prepared, after use of the formula, recording:*

   (a)   date and time of exchange;
   (b)   the formula used and exact wording of agreed variations;
   (c)   the completion date;
   (d)   the (balance) deposit to be paid;
   (e)   the identities of those involved in any conversation.

2.   *Those who are going to effect the exchange must first confirm the details in order to ensure that both parts are identical. This means in particular, that if either part of the contract has been amended since it was originally prepared, the solicitor who holds a part contract with the amendments must disclose them, so that it can be confirmed that the other part is similarly amended.*

9 July 1986, revised January 1996

Law Society telephone/fax/telex exchange – Formula C (1989)

Part I

The following is agreed:

Final time for exchange: [...] pm

Completion date:

Deposit to be paid to:

Each solicitor confirms that he or she holds a part of the contract in the agreed form signed by his or her client, or, if there is more than one client, by all of them. Each solicitor undertakes to the other that:

(a) he or she will continue to hold that part of the contract until the final time for exchange on the date the formula is used, and

(b) if the vendor's solicitor so notifies the purchaser's solicitor by fax, telephone or telex (whichever was previously agreed) by that time, they will both comply with part II of the formula.

The purchaser's solicitor further undertakes that either he or she or some other named person in his or her office will be available up to the final time for exchange to activate part II of the formula on receipt of the telephone call, fax or telex from the vendor's solicitors.

Part II

Each solicitor undertakes to the other henceforth to hold the part of the contract in his or her possession to the other's order, so that contracts are exchanged at that moment, and to despatch it to the other on that day. The purchaser's solicitor further undertakes to the vendor's solicitor to despatch on that day, or to arrange for the despatch on that day of, a banker's draft or a solicitor's client account cheque for the full deposit specified in the agreed form of contract (divided as the vendor's solicitor may have specified) to the vendor's solicitor and/or to some other solicitor whom the vendor's solicitor nominates, to be held on formula C terms.

'To despatch' means to send by first class post, or, where the other solicitor is a member of a document exchange (as to which the inclusion of a reference thereto in the solicitor's letterhead is to be conclusive evidence) by delivery to that or any other affiliated exchange, or by hand delivery direct to the recipient solicitor's office. 'Formula C terms' means that the deposit is held as stakeholder, or as agent for the vendor with authority to part with it only for the purpose of passing it to another solicitor as deposit in a related property purchase transaction on these terms.

Notes:

1.   *Two memoranda will be required when using formula C. One needs to record the use of part I, and a second needs to record the request of the vendor's solicitor to the purchaser's solicitor to activate part II.*

2.   *The first memorandum should record:*

    (a)   *the date and time when it was agreed to use formula C;*

    (b)   *the exact wording of any agreed variations;*

    (c)   *the final time, later that day, for exchange;*

    (d)   *the completion date;*

    (e)   *the name of the solicitor to whom the deposit was to be paid, or details of amounts and names if it was to be split; and*

    (f)   *the identities of those involved in any conversation.*

3.   *Formula C assumes the payment of a full contractual deposit (normally 10%).*

4.   *The contract term relating to the deposit must allow it to be passed on, with payment direct from payer to ultimate recipient, in the way in which the formula contemplates. The deposit must ultimately be held by a solicitor as stakeholder. Whilst some variation in the formula can be agreed this is a term of the formula which must not be varied, unless all the solicitors involved in the chain have agreed.*

5.   *If a buyer proposes to use a deposit guarantee policy, formula C will need substantial adaptation.*

6.   *It is essential prior to agreeing part I of formula C that those effecting the exchange ensure that both parts of the contract are identical.*

7.   *Using formula C involves a solicitor in giving a number of professional undertakings. These must be performed precisely. Any failure will be a serious breach of professional discipline. One of the undertakings may be to arrange that someone over whom the solicitor has no control will do something (i.e. to arrange for someone else to despatch the cheque or banker's draft in payment of the deposit). An undertaking is still binding even if it is to do something outside the solicitor's control.*

8.   *Solicitors do not as a matter of law have an automatic authority to exchange contracts on a formula C basis, and should always ensure that they have the client's express authority to use formula C. A suggested form of authority is set out below. It should be adapted to cover any special circumstances:*

I/We [...] understand that my/our sale and purchase of [...] are both part of a chain of linked property transactions, in which all parties want the security of contracts which become binding on the same day.

I/We agree that you should make arrangements with the other solicitors or licensed conveyancers involved to achieve this.

I/We understand that this involves each property-buyer offering, early on one day, to exchange contracts whenever, later that day, the seller so requests, and that the buyer's offer is on the basis that it cannot be withdrawn or varied during that day.

I/We agree that when I/we authorise you to exchange contracts, you may agree to exchange contracts on the above basis and give any necessary undertakings to the other parties involved in the chain and that my/our authority to you cannot be revoked throughout the day on which the offer to exchange contracts is made.

15 March 1989, revised January 1996

APPENDIX E

The Law Society Code for Completion by Post (2019)[1]

Warning: Use of this code embodies professional undertakings.

INTRODUCTION AND SCOPE

This code provides a voluntary procedure for postal completion for either residential or commercial transactions. It may also be used by those authorised by an appropriate professional body to undertake conveyancing. Solicitors adopting this code must be satisfied that its adoption will not be contrary to the interests of their client. When adopted, this code applies without variation unless otherwise agreed.

This code is intended to provide a fair balance of obligation between seller's and buyer's solicitors and to facilitate professional co-operation for the benefit of clients.

PROCEDURE

General

1. To adopt this code, both solicitors must agree, preferably in writing, to use it to complete a specific transaction, except that the use or adoption of the Law Society Conveyancing Protocol automatically implies use of this code unless otherwise stated in writing by either solicitor.
2. In this code:

    (i)   all references to the 'Seller' are references to the person or persons who will be at the point of completion entitled to convey the legal and/or equitable title to the property and

    (ii) all references to the 'Seller's Solicitor' are to the solicitor purporting to act for the party named as the seller in respect of the contract or purported contract that the buyer has entered into in order to acquire the property.

3. If the Seller's Solicitor has to withdraw from using this code, the buyer's solicitor should be notified of this not later than 4pm on the working day next before the completion date. If the Seller's Solicitor's authority to receive the monies is withdrawn later the buyer's solicitor must be notified immediately.
4. In complying with the terms of this code:

---

[1]   © The Law Society 2019.

(i) the Seller's Solicitor acts on completion as the buyer's solicitor's agent without fee or disbursement, but this obligation does not require the Seller's Solicitor to investigate or take responsibility for any breach of the seller's contractual obligations and is expressly limited to completion pursuant to paragraphs 11 to 13; and

(ii) where the Seller's Solicitor receives and/or holds the money received for completion, the Seller's Solicitor receives and/holds that money on trust for the person or persons who provided it, to be either

   (a) paid away only in respect of a completion in which the Seller executes and delivers a valid conveyance or transfer; or

   (b) repaid to the person who remitted it, if completion does not take place.

Before completion

5. The buyer's solicitor will use reasonable endeavours to ensure that enough funds are collected from the buyer and any mortgage lender in good time to transmit to the Seller's Solicitor on or before the completion date.

6. The Seller's Solicitor should provide to the buyer's solicitor replies to completion information, and undertakings in the Law Society's standard form, at least five working days before the completion date unless replies have been provided to such other form requesting completion information as may have been submitted by the buyer's solicitor.

7. The Seller's Solicitor will specify in writing to the buyer's solicitor the mortgages, charges or other financial incumbrances secured on the property which on or before completion are to be redeemed or discharged to the extent that they relate to the property, and by what method.

8. The Seller's Solicitor **undertakes**:

   (i) to have the Seller's authority to receive the purchase money on completion; and

   (ii) on completion, to have the authority of the proprietor of each mortgage, charge or other financial incumbrance which was specified under paragraph 7 but has not then been redeemed or discharged, to receive the sum intended to repay it;

   BUT if the Seller's Solicitor does not have all the necessary authorities then:

   (iii) to advise the buyer's solicitor no later than 4pm on the working day next before the completion date of the absence of those authorities or immediately if any is withdrawn later; and

   (iv) not to complete without the buyer's solicitor's instructions.

9. The buyer's solicitor may send the Seller's Solicitor instructions as to any other matters required by the buyer's solicitor which may include:

   (i) documents to be examined and marked;

   (ii) memoranda to be endorsed;

   (iii) undertakings to be given;

   (iv) deeds or other documents including transfers and any relevant undertakings and authorities relating to rents, deposits, keys, to be sent to the buyer's solicitor following completion;

   (v) consents, certificates or other authorities that may be required to deal with any restrictions on any Land Registry title to the property;

   (vi) executed Stock Transfer Forms relating to shares in any companies directly related to the conveyancing transaction.

10. The buyer's solicitor will remit to the Seller's Solicitor the sum required to complete, as notified in writing on the Seller's Solicitor's completion statement or otherwise in accordance with the contract, including any compensation payable for late completion

by reference to the 'contract rate' if either the Standard Conditions of Sale or the Standard Commercial Property Conditions are utilised, or, in default of notification, as shown by the contract. If the funds are remitted by transfer between banks, immediately upon becoming aware of their receipt, the Seller's Solicitor will report to the buyer's solicitor that the funds have been received.

Completion

11. The Seller's Solicitor will complete upon becoming aware of the receipt of the sum specified in paragraph 10, or a lesser sum should the buyer's solicitor and Seller's Solicitor so agree, unless

 (i) the buyer's solicitor has notified the Seller's Solicitor that the funds are to be held to the buyer's solicitor's order; or
 (ii) it has previously been agreed that completion is to take place at a later time.

 Any agreement or notification under this paragraph should if possible be made or confirmed in writing.

12. When completing, the Seller's Solicitor **undertakes**:

 (i) to comply with any agreed completion arrangements and any reasonable instructions given under paragraph 9;
 (ii) to redeem or obtain discharges for every mortgage, charge or other financial incumbrance specified under paragraph 7 so far as it relates to the property which has not already been redeemed or discharged;
 (iii) that the proprietor of each mortgage, charge or other financial incumbrance specified under paragraph 7 has been identified by the Seller's Solicitor to the extent necessary for the purpose of the buyer's solicitor's application to HM Land Registry.

After completion

13. The Seller's Solicitor **undertakes**:

 (i) immediately completion has taken place, to hold to the buyer's solicitor's order every document specified under paragraph 9 and not to exercise a lien over any of them;
 (ii) as soon as possible after completion:

 (a) to confirm to the buyer's solicitor by telephone, fax or email the date and time at which completion has taken place;
 (b) to notify the Seller's estate agent or other keyholder that completion has taken place, and authorise them to make keys available to the buyer immediately;

 (iii) as soon as possible after completion and in any event by the end of the working day following completion, to send *written confirmation that completion has taken place, and*, at the risk of the buyer's solicitor, the items specified under paragraph 9 to the buyer's solicitor by first class post or document exchange;
 (iv) if the discharge of any mortgage, charge or other financial incumbrance specified under paragraph 7 takes place by electronic means, to notify the buyer's solicitor as soon as confirmation is received from the proprietor of the mortgage, charge or other financial incumbrance that the discharge has taken or is taking place.

Supplementary

14. The rights and obligations of the parties, under the contract or otherwise, are not affected by this code and in the event of a conflict between the contract and this code, the contract shall prevail.
15. When someone authorised by an appropriate professional body to undertake conveyancing adopts this code, references to a 'solicitor' include that person.
16. A dispute or difference arising between solicitors who adopt this code (whether or not subject to any variation) relating directly to its application is to be referred to a single arbitrator agreed between the solicitors. If they do not agree on the appointment within one month, the President of the Law Society may appoint the arbitrator at the request of one of the solicitors.

NOTES TO THIS CODE

1. The 2019 edition of this code will apply to transactions where this code is adopted after the first day of May 2019.
2. The object of this code is to provide solicitors with a convenient means for completion on an agency basis when a representative of the buyer's solicitor is not attending at the office of the seller's solicitor.
3. As with the Law Society's formulae for exchange of contracts, this code embodies professional undertakings and is only recommended for adoption between solicitors and licensed conveyancers.
4. Paragraph 4(i) of this code provides that the Seller's Solicitor will act as agent for the buyer's solicitor without fee or disbursements. The convenience of not having to make a specific appointment on the date of completion for the buyer's solicitor to attend to complete personally will offset the agency work that the Seller's Solicitor has to do in completing under this code. Most solicitors will from time to time act for both sellers and buyers. If a Seller's Solicitor does consider that charges and/or disbursements are necessary in a particular case, this would represent a variation in this code and should be agreed in writing before exchange of contracts.
5. Paragraph 4(ii) of this code makes explicit the effect of the decisions in *Twinsectra Limited* v. *Yardley* [2002] UKHL 12, *Lloyds TSB Bank plc* v. *Markandan & Uddin (a firm)* [2012] EWCA Civ 65 and *P&P Property Limited* v. *Owen White & Catlin LLP and Dreamvar (UK) Limited* v. *Mishcon de Reya (a firm)* [2018] EWCA Civ 1082, that the Seller's Solicitor holds any purchase money received on trust for the person or persons who provided it and is under a fiduciary duty not to deal with that money other than in accordance with the terms of this code.
6. In view of the decision in *P&P Property Limited* v. *Owen White & Catlin LLP and Dreamvar (UK) Limited* v. *Mishcon de Reya (a firm)* [2018] EWCA Civ 1082, paragraph 8(i) of this code constitutes an undertaking that the Seller's Solicitor has authority from the true owner of the title to the property named in the contract to receive the purchase money, and that such person is at the point of completion entitled to convey such title as the contract states will be conferred. This case law is also reflected in the definition of 'Seller' used throughout this code.
7. In view of the decision in *Edward Wong Finance Company Limited* v. *Johnson, Stokes and Master* [1984] AC 296, paragraph 8(ii) of this code requires the Seller's Solicitor to undertake on completion to have the authority of the proprietor of every mortgage or charge to be redeemed to receive the sum needed to repay such charge. Such an undertaking remains an indispensable component of residential conveyancing. While the Seller's Solicitor will often not be specifically instructed by the Seller's mortgagee, the course of dealings between the solicitor and mortgagee in relation to the monies required to redeem the mortgage should at the very least evidence implicit authority

from the mortgagee to the solicitor to receive the sum required to repay the charge (if, for example, the mortgagee has given its bank details to the solicitor for transmission of the redemption funds).

On the basis of those dealings (and in the absence of any contrary statements from the mortgagee), the Seller's Solicitor should be in a position to give the undertaking to discharge (in the Law Society's recommended form, adapted where relevant for electronic discharges) and, for paper discharges (DS1, etc.), to undertake that they have identified the Seller's mortgagee to the extent necessary for the purpose of the buyer's solicitor's application to the Land Registry, on which the buyer's solicitor should be able to rely.

The Seller's Solicitor should, if at all possible, receive an express confirmation from the Seller's mortgagee that the paper discharge, or an acknowledgment of discharge (for electronic discharges) will be supplied to them. If the Seller's mortgagee expressly prohibits the Seller's Solicitor from dealing with the redemption money, the Seller's Solicitor should notify the buyer's solicitor as soon as possible. The Seller's Solicitor and buyer's solicitor should consider whether in those circumstances they can adopt this code and, if so, the necessary variations.

8. In view of the decisions in *Angel Solicitors (a firm)* v. *Jenkins O'Dowd & Barth* [2009] EWHC 46 (Ch) and *Clark* v. *Lucas LLP* [2009] EWHC 1952 (Ch), the undertaking in paragraph 12(ii) of this code is to be taken, unless otherwise stated, as including confirmation that a satisfactory redemption statement has been obtained from the lender whose charge is to be redeemed.

9. Paragraph 14 of this code provides that nothing in this code overrides any rights and obligations of the parties under the contract or otherwise.

10. The Seller's Solicitor is to inform the buyer's solicitor of the mortgages or charges which will be redeemed or discharged (see paragraph 7 of this code). The information may be given in reply to completion information and undertakings (see paragraph 6 of this code). Such a reply may also amount to an undertaking.

11. Care must be taken if there is a sale and sub-sale. The sub-Seller's Solicitor may not hold the transfer nor be in a position to receive the funds required to discharge the Seller's mortgage on the property. Enquiries should be made to ascertain if the monies or some of the monies payable on completion should, with the authority of either the sub-Seller or the sub-Seller's Solicitor, be sent direct to the Seller's Solicitor and not to the sub-Seller's solicitor.

12. Care must also be taken if there is a simultaneous resale and completion. Enquiries should be made by the ultimate buyer's solicitor of the intermediate Seller's Solicitor as to the price being paid on that purchase. Having appointed the intermediate Seller's Solicitor as agent, the buyer's solicitor is fixed with the knowledge of an agent even without having personal knowledge.

13. For the purposes of paragraphs 10 and 13 of this code, as it will be in the best interests of the client to know as soon as possible that completion has taken place, it is assumed that procedures promptly to notify the arrival of monies will be in place.

14. Any variation of this code must be agreed in writing before completion.

15. These notes form part of this code and this code is to be construed by reference to them. These notes refer only to some of the points in this code that practitioners may wish to consider before agreeing to adopt it.

APPENDIX F

Law Society and Council of Mortgage Lenders approved certificate of title[1]

ANNEX

CERTIFICATE OF TITLE

Details box

TO: (Lender)	
Lender's Reference or Account No:	
The Borrower:	
Property:	
Title Number:	
Mortgage Advance:	
Price stated in transfer:	
Completion Date:	
Conveyancer's Name & Address:	
Conveyancer's Reference:	
Conveyancer's bank, sort code and account number:	
Date of instructions:	

WE THE CONVEYANCERS NAMED ABOVE CERTIFY as follows:

(1) If so instructed, we have checked the identity of the Borrower (and anyone else required to sign the mortgage deed or other document connected with the mortgage) by reference to the document or documents precisely specified in writing by you.

(2) Except as otherwise disclosed to you in writing:

(i) we have investigated the title to the Property, we are not aware of any other

---

[1] Agreed between the Law Society and the Council of Mortgage Lenders [now UK Finance] to be used from and including 30 November 2015.

financial charges secured on the Property which will affect the Property after completion of the mortgage and, upon completion of the mortgage, both you and the mortgagor (whose identity has been checked in accordance with paragraph (1) above) will have a good and marketable title to the Property and to appurtenant rights free from prior mortgages or charges and from onerous encumbrances which title will be registered with absolute title;

(ii)   we have compared the extent of the Property shown on any plan provided by you against relevant plans in the title deeds and/or the description of the Property in any valuation which you have supplied to us, and in our opinion there are no material discrepancies;

(iii) the assumptions stated by the valuer about the title (its tenure, easements, boundaries and restrictions on use) in any valuation which you have supplied to us are correct;

(iv)   if the Property is leasehold the terms of the lease accord with your instructions, including any requirements you have for covenants by the Landlord and/or a management company and/or by a deed of mutual covenant for the insurance, repair and maintenance of the structure, exterior and common parts of any building of which the Property forms part, and we have or will obtain on or before completion a clear receipt for the last payment of rent and service charge;

(v)   if the Property is a commonhold unit, the commonhold community statement contains the terms specified by you and does not include any restrictions on occupation or use specified by you as unacceptable, and we have or will obtain on or before completion a commonhold unit information certificate;

(vi)   we have made reasonable enquiries to satisfy ourselves that buildings insurance has been arranged for the property from no later than completion. We have reminded the borrower that buildings insurance must be in place in accordance with the terms of your mortgage offer by completion and that buildings insurance cover must be maintained throughout the mortgage term;

(vii) if the Property is to be purchased by the Borrower:

(a)   the contract for sale provides for vacant possession on completion;

(b)   the seller has owned or been the registered owner of the Property for not less than six months; and

(c)   we are not acting on behalf of the seller;

(viii) we are in possession of:

(a)   either a local search or local search insurance; and

(b)   such other searches or search insurance as are appropriate to the Property, the mortgagor and any guarantor, in each case in accordance with your instructions;

(ix)   nothing has been revealed by our searches and enquiries which would prevent the Property being used by any occupant for residential purposes; and

(x)   neither any principal nor any other individual in the firm giving this certificate nor any spouse, child, parent, brother or sister of such a person is interested in the Property (whether alone or jointly with any other) as mortgagor.

WE:

(a)   undertake, prior to use of the mortgage advance, to obtain in the form required by you the execution of a mortgage and a guarantee as appropriate by the persons whose identities have been checked in accordance with paragraph (1) above as those of the Borrower, any other person in whom the legal estate is vested and any guarantor; and, if required by you:

     (i)   to obtain their signatures to the forms of undertaking required by you in relation to the use, occupation or physical state of the Property;

     (ii)   to ask the Borrower for confirmation that the information about occupants given in your mortgage instructions or offer is correct; and

     (iii) to obtain consents in the form required by you from any existing or prospective occupier(s) aged 17 or over of the Property specified by you or of whom we are aware;

(b) have made or will make such Bankruptcy, Land Registry or Land Charges Searches as may be necessary to justify certificate no. (2)(i) above;

(c) will within the period of protection afforded by the searches referred to in paragraph (b) above:

     (i)   complete the mortgage;

     (ii)   arrange for the issue of a stamp duty land tax certificate if appropriate;

     (iii) deliver to the Land Registry electronically or physically the documents necessary to register the mortgage in your favour and any relevant prior dealings; and

     (iv) effect any other registrations necessary to protect your interests as mortgagee;

(d) will despatch to you such deeds and documents relating to the Property as you require with a list of them in the form prescribed by you within ten working days of receipt by us of the title information document from the Land Registry;

(e) will not part with the mortgage advance (and will return it to you if required) if it shall come to our notice prior to completion that the Property will at completion be occupied in whole or in part otherwise than in accordance with your instructions;

(f)   will not accept instructions, except with your consent in writing, to prepare any lease or tenancy agreement relating to the Property or any part of it prior to despatch of the title information document to you;

(g) will not use the mortgage advance until satisfied that, prior to or contemporaneously with the transfer of the Property to the mortgagor, there will be discharged:

     (i)   any existing mortgage on property the subject of an associated sale of which we are aware; and

     (ii)   any other mortgages made by a lender identified by you secured against a property located in England or Wales where you have given either an account number or numbers or a property address;

(h) will notify you in writing if any matter comes to our attention before completion which would render the certificate given above untrue or inaccurate and, in those circumstances, will defer completion pending your authority to proceed and will return the mortgage advance to you if required; and

(i)   confirm that we have complied, or will comply, with your instructions in all other respects to the extent that they do not extend beyond the limitations set out below).

Types of instruction which may be accepted

If acting for both lender and Borrower in a standard mortgage, you and the individual conducting or supervising the transaction may only accept or act upon instructions from the lender which are limited to the following matters:

(a) (i)   taking reasonable steps to check the identity of the borrower (and anyone else required to sign the mortgage deed or other document connected with the mortgage) by reference to a document or documents, such as a passport, precisely specified in writing by the lender;

(ii) following the guidance given by the Law Society or the Solicitors Regulation Authority on property fraud and on money laundering;

(iii) checking that the seller's conveyancers (if unknown to you) appear in a current legal directory or hold practising certificates issued by their professional body; and

(iv) in the case of a lender with no branch office within reasonable proximity of the borrower, carrying out the money laundering checks precisely specified in writing by the lender;

(b) making appropriate searches relating to the property in public registers (for example, local searches, commons registration searches, mining searches), and reporting any results specified by the lender or which you consider may adversely affect the lender; or effecting search insurance;

(c) making enquiries on legal matters relating to the property reasonably specified by the lender, and reporting the replies;

(d) reporting the purchase price stated in the transfer and on how the borrower says that the purchase money (other than the mortgage advance) is to be provided; and reporting if you will not have control over the payment of all the purchase money (other than a deposit paid to an estate agent or a reservation fee paid to a builder or developer);

(e) reporting if the seller or the Borrower (if the property is already owned by the Borrower) has not owned or been the registered owner of the property for at least six months;

(f) making reasonable enquiries that buildings insurance has been arranged for the property from no later than completion and reminding the Borrower that the buildings insurance must be in place in accordance with the terms of the mortgage offer by completion and that buildings insurance cover must be maintained throughout the term;

(g) investigating title to the property and appurtenant rights; reporting any defects revealed, advising on the need for any consequential statutory declarations or indemnity insurance, and approving and effecting indemnity cover if required by the lender; and reporting if you are aware of any rights needed for the use or enjoyment of the property over other land;

(h) reporting on any financial charges (for example, improvement or repair grants or Housing Act discounts) secured on the property revealed by your searches and enquiries which will affect the property after completion of the mortgage;

(i) in the case of a leasehold property:

(i) confirming that the lease contains the terms stipulated by the lender and does not include any terms specified by the lender as unacceptable;

(ii) obtaining a suitable deed of variation or indemnity insurance if the terms of the lease are unsatisfactory;

(iii) enquiring of the seller or the borrower (if the property is already owned by the Borrower) as to any known breaches of covenant by the landlord or any superior landlord and reporting any such breaches to the lender;

(iv) reporting if you become aware of the landlord's absence or insolvency;

(v) making a company search and checking the last three years' published accounts of any management company with responsibilities under the lease;

(vi) if the Borrower is required to be a shareholder in the management company, complying with the lender's requirements on obtaining share certificates, stock transfer forms and other related documentation;

(vii) obtaining any necessary consent to or prior approval of the assignment and mortgage;

(viii) obtaining a clear receipt for the last payment of rent and service charge. If

136

confirmation of payment from the landlord cannot be obtained, obtaining confirmation from the seller that there are no breaches of the terms of the lease and being satisfied that the security will not be prejudiced by the absence of such a receipt; and

(ix) serving notice of the assignment and mortgage on the landlord;

(j) in the case of a commonhold unit:

   (i) confirming receipt of satisfactory evidence that common parts insurance is in place for at least the sum required by the lender and covers the risks specified by the lender;

   (ii) confirming that the commonhold community statement contains the terms specified by the lender and does not include any restrictions on occupation or use specified by the lender as unacceptable;

   (iii) enquiring of the seller (or the borrower if the property is already owned by the Borrower) and the commonhold association as to any known breaches of the commonhold community statement by the commonhold association or any unit-holder, and reporting any such breaches to the lender;

   (iv) making a company search to verify that the commonhold association is in existence and remains registered, and that there is no registered indication that it is to be wound up;

   (v) obtaining the last three years' published accounts of the commonhold association and reporting any apparent problems with the association to the lender;

   (vi) obtaining a commonhold unit information certificate; and

   (vii) serving notice of the transfer and mortgage of the commonhold unit on the commonhold association;

(k) if the property is subject to a letting, checking that the type of letting and its terms comply with the lender's requirements;

(l) making appropriate pre-completion searches, including a bankruptcy search against the Borrower, any other person in whom the legal estate is vested and any guarantor;

(m) receiving, releasing and transmitting the mortgage advance, including asking for any final inspection needed and dealing with any retentions and cashbacks;

(n) procuring execution of the mortgage deed and form of guarantee as appropriate by the persons whose identities have been checked in accordance with any requirements of the lender under (a) above as those of the borrower, any other person in whom the legal estate is vested and any guarantor; obtaining their signatures to the forms of undertaking required by the lender in relation to the use, occupation or physical state of the property; and complying with the lender's requirements if any document is to be executed under a power of attorney;

(o) asking the Borrower for confirmation that the information about occupants given in the mortgage instructions or offer is correct; obtaining consents in the form required by the lender from existing or prospective occupiers of the property aged 17 or over specified by the lender, or of whom you are aware;

(p) advising the Borrower on the terms of any document required by the lender to be signed by the borrower;

(q) advising any other person required to sign any document on the terms of that document or, if there is a conflict of interests between that person and the borrower or the lender, advising that person on the need for separate legal advice and arranging for them to see an independent conveyancer;

(r) obtaining the legal transfer of the property to the mortgagor;

(s) procuring the redemption of:

   (i) existing mortgages on property the subject of any associated sale of which you are aware; and

(ii)   any other mortgages secured against a property located in England or Wales made by an identified lender where an identified account number or numbers or a property address has been given by the lender;

(t)   ensuring the redemption or postponement of existing mortgages on the property, and registering the mortgage with the priority required by the lender;

(u)   making administrative arrangements in relation to any collateral security, such as an endowment policy, or in relation to any collateral warranty or guarantee relating to the physical condition of the property, such as NHBC documentation;

(v)   registering the transfer and mortgage;

(w)   giving legal advice on any matters reported on under 2.3 suggesting courses of action open to the lender, and complying with the lender's instructions on the action to be taken;

(x)   disclosing any relationship specified by the lender between you and the borrower;

(y)   storing safely the title deeds and documents pending registration and delivery to or as directed by the lender; and

(z)   retaining the information contained in your conveyancing file for at least six years from the date of the mortgage.

OUR duties to you are limited to the matters set out in this certificate and we accept no further liability or responsibility whatsoever. The payment by you to us (by whatever means) of the mortgage advance or any part of it constitutes acceptance of this limitation and any assignment to you by the Borrower of any rights of action against us to which the Borrower may be entitled shall take effect subject to this limitation.

Signature box

SIGNED on behalf of THE CONVEYANCERS:
NAME of Authorised Signatory:
QUALIFICATION of Authorised Signatory:
DATE of Signature:

Solicitors Regulation Authority warning notice on undertakings[1]

Important: The content below was written and issued before the introduction of the SRA Handbook on 6 October 2011 and may refer to regulatory material that is no longer in effect. For further information, please contact our Professional Ethics helpline.

The SRA takes breaches of undertakings very seriously.

Your obligations are set out in rules 1, 5.01 and 10.05 of the Solicitors' Code of Conduct 2007 and its guidance.

Many transactions depend on the use of undertakings enabling you to negotiate and conduct your client's business successfully.

Where you give an undertaking

Those placing reliance on it will expect you to fulfil it. Ensure your undertakings are:
- Specific
- Measurable
- Agreed
- Realistic
- Timed

A breach of undertaking can lead to a disciplinary finding and costs direction.

Undertakings you give are also summarily enforceable by the High Court. Be aware that you do not become exposed to a liability within the excess of your firm's insurance.

Where you accept an undertaking

Ensure that in doing so your client's position is protected and you are not exposed to a breach.

If you are a regulated person or firm

- Be clear about who can give undertakings.
- Ensure all staff understand they need your client's agreement.
- Be clear about how compliance will be monitored.
- Maintain a central record to ensure and monitor compliance.
- Prescribe the manner in which undertakings may be given.
- Prepare standard undertakings, where possible, with clear instructions that any departure be authorised in accordance with supervision and management responsibilities.
- Adopt a system that ensures terms are checked by another fee-earner.
- Confirm oral undertakings (given or received) in writing.

---

[1] © The Law Society 2009. Last updated by the Solicitors Regulation Authority April 2009.

- Copy each undertaking and attach it to the relevant file; label the file itself.
- Ensure all staff understand the undertakings they give when using the Law Society's formulae for exchange of contracts and its code for completion by post.

To report to us on a confidential basis, contact our Red Alert line.

For advice, contact our Professional Ethics helpline.

Mortgage fraud practice note[1]

Criminals will exploit weaknesses in lending and conveyancing systems to gain illegitimate financial advantage from the UK property market.

This can be either:

- opportunistic action using misrepresentation of income or property value to obtain greater loans than a person is entitled to, or
- organised crime syndicates overvaluing properties, using false identities and failing to make any mortgage repayments.

A solicitor will be involved in most property transactions undertaken in the UK. You can find yourself criminally liable if your client commits mortgage fraud, because of the extension of the definition of fraud in the Fraud Act 2006 and the anti-money laundering regime in the UK.

You can be liable even if you were not aware of the fraud or did not actively participate in it.

Courts will assume a high level of knowledge and education on your part. They will often be less willing to accept claims that you were unwittingly involved if you have not applied appropriate due diligence.

This practice note highlights the warning signs of mortgage fraud and outlines how you can protect yourself and your firm from being used to commit mortgage fraud.

LEGAL STATUS

This practice note is the Law Society's view of good practice in this area. It is not legal advice.

Practice notes are issued by the Law Society for the use and benefit of its members. They represent the Law Society's view of good practice in a particular area. They are not intended to be the only standard of good practice that solicitors can follow. You are not required to follow them, but doing so will make it easier to account to oversight bodies for your actions.

Practice notes are not legal advice, nor do they necessarily provide a defence to complaints of misconduct or of inadequate professional service. While care has been taken to ensure that they are accurate, up to date and useful, the Law Society will not accept any legal liability in relation to them.

For queries or comments on this practice note contact the Law Society's Practice Advice Service.

PROFESSIONAL CONDUCT

The following sections of the SRA Handbook are relevant to mortgage fraud:

- Principle 1 – Uphold the Rule of Law and the Administration of Justice
- Chapter 3 – Conflicts of Interest
- Chapter 4 – Confidentiality and disclosure

---

[1]   © The Law Society. This practice note is as stated on 11 February 2019. Practice notes are updated by the Law Society from time to time. Solicitors are advised to check **www.lawsociety. org.uk** for the latest version.

SRA PRINCIPLES

There are ten mandatory principles which apply to all those the SRA regulates and to all aspects of practice. The principles can be found in the SRA Handbook.

The principles apply to solicitors or managers of authorised bodies who are practising from an office outside the UK. They also apply if you are a lawyer-controlled body practising from an office outside the UK.

TERMINOLOGY

Must – A specific requirement in legislation or of a principle, rule, outcome or other mandatory provision in the SRA Handbook. You must comply, unless there are specific exemptions or defences provided for in relevant legislation or the SRA Handbook.

Should – Outside of a regulatory context, good practice for most situations in the Law Society's view. In the case of the SRA Handbook, an indicative behaviour or other non-mandatory provision (such as may be set out in notes or guidance).

These may not be the only means of complying with legislative or regulatory requirements and there may be situations where the suggested route is not the best possible route to meet the needs of your client. However, if you do not follow the suggested route, you should be able to justify to oversight bodies why the alternative approach you have taken is appropriate, either for your practice, or in the particular retainer.

May – A non-exhaustive list of options for meeting your obligations or running your practice. Which option you choose is determined by the profile of the individual practice, client or retainer. You may be required to justify why this was an appropriate option to oversight bodies.

The Law Society also provides a full glossary of other terms used throughout this practice note [**www.lawsociety.org.uk/for-the-public/legal-glossary**].

1 INTRODUCTION

1.1 Who should read this practice note?

All solicitors who do conveyancing work involving a mortgage. Solicitors responsible for supervising others doing conveyancing work should ensure those staff have read this practice note.

1.2 What is the issue?

Criminals will exploit weaknesses in lending and conveyancing systems to gain illegitimate financial advantage from the UK property market. This can be either:

- opportunistic action using misrepresentation of income or property value to obtain greater loans than a person is entitled to, or
- organised crime syndicates overvaluing properties, using false identities and failing to make any mortgage repayments.

A solicitor will be involved in most property transactions undertaken in the UK. You can find yourself criminally liable if your client commits mortgage fraud, because of the extension of the definition of fraud in the Fraud Act 2006 and the anti-money laundering regime in the UK.

You can be liable even if you were not aware of the fraud or actively participated in it.

Courts will assume a high level of knowledge and education on your part. They will often be less willing to accept claims that you were unwittingly involved if you have not applied appropriate due diligence.

This practice note highlights the warning signs of mortgage fraud and outlines how you can protect yourself and your firm from being used to commit mortgage fraud.

2   HOW DOES MORTGAGE FRAUD OCCUR?

2.1   What is mortgage fraud?

Mortgage fraud occurs where individuals defraud a financial institution or private lender through the mortgage process.

The definition of fraud in the Fraud Act 2006 covers fraud by false representation and by failure to disclose information where there is a legal duty to disclose.

False representations can be made explicitly or implicitly and may occur even where you know only that the representation might be misleading or untrue.

The money obtained through fraud will be the proceeds of crime. Under the Proceeds of Crime Act 2002 as amended, you risk committing a money laundering offence if you acquire, use, have possession of, enter into an arrangement with respect to, or transfer this criminal property, or if you suspect money laundering.

Read the relevant legislation and the Legal Sector Affinity Group Anti-money Laundering Guidance.

Read the joint Law Society and Land Registry advice note on property and title fraud issued in September 2017.

2.2   Opportunistic mortgage fraud

2.2.1   *General methodology*

Individual purchasers can commit mortgage fraud by obtaining a higher mortgage than they are entitled to by providing untrue or misleading information or failing to disclose required information. This may include providing incorrect information about:

- identity
- income
- employment
- other debt obligations
- the sources of funds other than the mortgage for the purchase
- the value of the property
- the price to be paid and whether any payments have been, or will be made, directly between the seller and the purchaser

2.2.2   *Use of professionals*

Opportunistic fraudsters will not usually attempt to include their solicitor in the original fraud. However, you may become aware of information conflicting with that provided to the lender as you progress the conveyance.

Clients engaged in opportunistic fraud may be evasive when questioned on the conflict and may try to dissuade you from conducting relevant checks or advising the lender.

2.3 Large scale mortgage fraud

2.3.1 General methodology

Large scale mortgage fraud is usually more sophisticated and involves several properties. It may be committed by criminal groups or individuals, referred to herein as fraudsters.

The buy-to-let market is particularly vulnerable to mortgage fraud, whether through new-build apartment complexes or large-scale renovation projects. Occasionally, commercial properties will be involved. The common steps are:

- The nominated purchasers taking out the mortgage often have no beneficial interest in the property, and may even be fictitious.
- The property value is inflated and the mortgage will be sought for the full inflated valuation.
- Mortgage payments are often not met and the properties are allowed to deteriorate or used for other criminal or fraudulent activities, including drug production, people trafficking, unlicensed gambling and prostitution.
- When the bank seeks payment of the mortgage, the fraudsters raise mortgages with another bank through further fictitious purchasers and effectively sell the property back to themselves, but at an even greater leveraged valuation.
- Because the second mortgage is inflated, the first mortgage and arrears are paid off, leaving a substantial profit. This may be repeated many times
- Eventually a bank forecloses on the property, only to find it in disrepair and worth significantly less than the current mortgage and its arrears.

2.3.2 Use of non-bank lenders

Fraudsters may use private sources of funding such as property clubs, especially when credit market conditions tighten. These lenders often have lower safeguards than institutional lenders, leaving them vulnerable to organised fraud.

Property clubs can be targeted particularly in relation to overseas properties where the property either does not exist, or it is a vacant piece of land, not a developed property.

2.3.3 Use of corporate structures

Sometimes fraud is achieved by selling the property between related private companies, rather than between fictitious individuals. The transactions will involve inflated values, and will not be at arm's length.

Increasingly, off-shore companies are being used, with the property sold several times within the group before approaching a lender for a mortgage at an inflated value.

You may be asked to act for both the seller and the purchaser in these transactions.

2.3.4 Flipping and back-to-back transactions

Investors will always look to re-sell a property at a profit. However, fraudsters may seek to re-sell a property very quickly for a substantially increased price.

This process is called 'flipping', and will usually involve back-to-back sales of the property to limit the time between sales. Variations on this fraud include:

- The first mortgage is not registered against the property, and not redeemed upon completion of the second sale.
- The second purchaser may be fictitious, using a false identity or be someone vulnerable to pressure from the fraudster.

- A mortgage may only be obtained by the second purchaser and for an amount significantly higher than the value of the property. The profit goes to the fraudster.

2.3.5   Use of professionals

Fraudsters will usually use at least one professional at the core of the fraud, to direct and reassure other professionals acting at the periphery. Mortgage brokers and introducers have been used in this role in the past.

Mortgage lenders often rely on other professionals to verify the legitimacy of a transaction and safeguard their interests. Lenders may not extensively verify information they receive, especially in a rising market.

Institutional lenders will subscribe to the Council of Mortgage Lenders' Handbook [UK Finance Mortgage Lenders' Handbook] and expect solicitors to comply with these guidelines. Private investors will rely on compliance with the SRA Handbook to protect their lending.

You may be approached in any of the following ways:

- You may be asked to complete the transaction and simply transfer the title in accordance with already exchanged contracts. Explanations are often given about former solicitors being unable to act due to delay or not being on the new lender's mortgage panel. A lender who has received the loan applications and already approved the loan may approach you with packaged transactions and completed paper work.
- You may be encouraged to alter the value or give other misleading information on the Certificate of Title given to the lender.
- You may be encouraged not to comply with obligations in the CML Lenders Handbook or the BSA Mortgage Instructions.
- You may be offered continued work at a higher margin to encourage less diligent checks.
- Fraudsters may attempt to recruit you into the fraud, especially if you have unwittingly assisted previously, or have developed an especially close relationship with other participants in the scheme.

2.4   Other methodologies

Fraud methodologies regularly evolve, particularly in changing economic circumstances.

2.4.1   Equity release fraud

Where clients are struggling to meet mortgage repayments, they may turn to an equity release scheme to be able to remain in their homes.

This scheme sees home owners receiving an offer from a third party to purchase the property while the home owner is allowed to rent the property. The home owner is given the option to purchase the property back when their financial position improves.

However, criminal involvement can result in the following:

1. The home owner sells the property to someone who is actually a member of the criminal syndicate, a mortgage mule, or an entirely fictitious person.
2. A mortgage will be taken out by this investor for an inflated value against the property.
3. The original loan will be paid out and the money representing the equity in the home will be taken by the criminal syndicate. No payments will be made towards the mortgage.
4. The original home owner will be unaware of the lack of payments being made until the bank seeks to repossess the property and evicts them a mere tenant.

5.   The value of the mortgage will be far greater than the original mortgage and it will be impossible for the original owner to purchase the property back.

2.4.2   Application hijack

Application hijacking involves criminals intervening before completion of a mortgage, falsely claiming to be the new representatives for the purchaser. They thereby obtain the mortgage advance in place of the real purchaser.

The lender is contacted later by the real representatives looking to complete the transaction, only to find the funds have already been paid away and have now disappeared.

The criminals will generally pose as solicitors or conveyancers, taking the details of someone who is on the professional register. They will then use fake or cloned letterhead to write to the lender as the representative, providing their own account details for the client account.

Solicitors who have unknowingly undertaken work for criminal syndicates previously may find that they are at greater risk of this type of fraud as the syndicate will have access to their genuine letter head and standard mortgage correspondence.

2.4.3   After the event mortgaging

While re-mortgaging and re-financing may be common practices, the use of apparent equity to access mortgage funds is an avenue also exploited by criminals.

Fraudsters will use private funds, often of criminal origin, to purchase a property. Often the purchase will be through an auction and may involve repossessed properties, to ensure a discounted purchase price.

After the purchase is completed, and usually within 12 months, the fraudster will seek external funding against the property.

They then take the mortgage advance and disappear, failing to make any payments.

Another variation on this methodology is that the fraudster will pose as a property developer and will seek bridging loans to cover the purchase of a number of properties. These may be properties which the fraudsters previously used as part of a flipping scheme and have finally been repossessed by the bank.

The bridging loan is only sought after the purchase has been registered and possession has been taken of the property.

2.4.4   Claiming deceased estates

Criminals will make use of the notices section of their local papers to identify deceased estates that can be exploited for criminal gain, either because there are no known heirs or probate has been delayed.

They will seek to either falsely establish their identity as a long-lost heir or will pose as the deceased person. In both scenarios, they will seek a mortgage over the existing equity in the property and then disappear with the funds.

2.4.5   Court orders for sale

Properties that have been repossessed or are unable to be sold are left unoccupied and boarded up.

1.   Criminals will seek out these properties and details of the owners.
2.   They will then apply to the County Court for a judgment against the owner over a non-existent debt.
3.   They will not actually give the owner notice of this application.

4. Once obtained, this judgment is converted into an order for sale.
5. The property is sold either directly to the person claiming the debt or to one of their associates at an inflated price, using criminal money.
6. A mortgage will be obtained over the property at the inflated value.
7. The mortgage advance will be taken and no payments will be made.

3   WARNING SIGNS

Criminal methodologies are continually changing. However, there are several known warning signs, which may be indicators of mortgage fraud.

You should remain alert to warning signs in the information and documentation which are in your possession. You should pay particular attention to transactions which exhibit a number of warning signs.

3.1   Identity and ownership

- The client or the property involved is located a long distance from your firm. If bulk long-distance instructions are not in your normal work, you may ask why they chose your firm, especially if they are a new client.
- The client seems unusually uninterested in their purchase. You should look for other warning signs suggesting they are not the real purchaser.
- The seller is a private company or they have recently purchased the property from a private company. You should consider whether the office holders or shareholders of the private company are otherwise connected with the transaction you are undertaking, and whether this is an arm's length commercial transaction.
- The client does not usually engage in property investment of this scale. You should ask why they are undertaking this new venture and where they are getting the financial backing from.
- The client, according to the Property Register, has owned the property for many years but has very limited or vague knowledge of it, especially when any enquiry is raised.
- The current owner has owned the property for under six months. You should ask them to explain why they are selling so quickly.
- The client's credit history is shorter than you would expect for their age, when you run an electronic identity check, which may include credit history information. Fraudsters will often run a fake identity for a few months to give it legitimacy. You should ask your client about this.
- There are plans for a sub-sale or back-to-back transactions. You should ask your client why they are structuring the transaction this way and seek information on the identities of the second purchaser, their solicitor and the lender.
- There is a last minute change of representative on the other side.
- A party unrelated to the transaction is paying your fees.
- The property has a history of being re-sold quickly or mortgages settled quickly.
- A transfer of title to land is requested with respect to only some of the seller's holdings and the properties are not grouped together.
- Finance is sought after the property has been registered in the buyer's name.
- The property has been registered to an owner for a significant period of time and the person claiming to be the owner does not appear to be of an age to have held the land for that length of time.
- The other conveyancer or solicitor allegedly involved in the transaction has an e-mail address from a large-scale web based provider.
- There is a County Court judgment against the property.
- The land is transferred following a court order, but the mortgage is sought some time later.

147

3.2 Value

- The property value has significantly increased in a short period of time out of line with the market in the area.
- The mortgage is for the full property value. This should be considered in light of the other warning signs.
- The seller or developer have provided incentives, allowances or discounts. These may include cash back, free holidays, household fittings, payment of legal fees, help with mortgage repayments or rental guarantees, among others. You should consider whether this information has been properly disclosed to the lender.
- The deposit is being paid by someone other than the purchaser. You should ask why, where the money is coming from, and whether this information has been properly disclosed to the lender.
- The purchaser has paid the deposit directly to the seller or a developer. You should ask for evidence of the payment and consider whether this information has been properly disclosed to the lender.
- There is money left over from the mortgage after the purchase price has been paid, and you are asked to pay this money to the account of someone you do not know, or to the introducer. You should ask why, and remember that you must not use your client account as a mere banking facility. See note ix to Rule 14(5) of the SRA Accounts Rules 2011 and Guidance Note 5.
- You are asked to enter a price on the title that is greater than you know was paid for the property. You should ask why the prices are different.
- There has been a recent transfer of land where no money has changed hands or the price was significantly less than the full market value or the value now stated.
- The valuation of or payment for chattels with the sale appears high.

4   PROTECTING YOUR FIRM

4.1   Ask questions

You should ask questions if you receive unusual instructions from your client, if any of the warning signs are present, or there are inconsistencies in the retainer. You will better understand your instructions and be able to effectively assess the risk of the retainer to your firm.

Criminal methodologies change constantly, so you should remain alert to transactions that are unusual for a normal residential or commercial conveyance.

4.2   Identify and verify the client

You must find out and verify the identity of your client and, where relevant, any beneficial owners. This is important whether you are acting for the purchaser or the seller.

You are not expected to be experts in forged documents, but you should ensure the identities you have been given correspond with the information on the mortgage documents and the bank accounts relating to the transaction.

If you have concerns about a person's identity, you should consider checking whether the person is listed on a negative database, such as the register of deaths or a list of known fraudsters.

Where a private company is the seller, or the seller has purchased from a private company in the recent past, and you are concerned that the sale may not be an arm's length transaction, you should conduct a search of the Companies Register.

You should find out the names and addresses of the office holders, the shareholders and persons with significant control, which can be cross referenced with the names of those connected with the transaction, the seller and the buyer. You should check dates shown on the Companies search.

You should consider the Legal Sector Affinity Group Anti-money Laundering Guidance, the joint Land Registry and Law Society practice note on property and title fraud, UK Finance Lenders' Handbook and BSA mortgage instructions when deciding that information needs to be obtained to identify and verify the clients and others.

4.2.1   Enhanced due diligence

Many mortgage fraudsters provide only paperwork and try to avoid meetings, particularly with the named purchasers.

If you do not meet your client in a property transaction, you must take this into account when assessing whether the situation presents a higher risk of money laundering, requiring the application of enhanced due diligence, in accordance with the Money Laundering, Terrorist Financing and Transfer of Funds (Information on the Payer) Regulations 2017 (Money Laundering Regulations).

Read about enhanced due diligence in the Legal Sector Affinity Group Anti-money Laundering Guidance, chapter 4.12.

4.2.2   Reliance

Fraudsters will try to limit scrutiny of their identity and the transaction. They may ask you to use the reliance provisions under the Money Laundering Regulations to minimise the number of due diligence checks that you conduct.

You should consider reliance as a potential risk in itself. You remain liable for any breach of the regulations if the checks you rely on have not been conducted properly. To protect your firm, you should ask the following questions of the firm or individual you are being asked to rely on:

- Are they regulated for anti-money laundering purposes? Mortgage brokers are currently not supervised under the Money Laundering Regulations.
- Have you done business with them previously?
- Are they from an established firm?
- What is their reputation? A general web search may reveal this.
- Are they able to provide you with the client due diligence material they have?

You should ask for copies of the due diligence conducted, so that you can cross reference documents within the retainer and satisfy yourself as to the identity of the purchaser and, where relevant, beneficial owners.

Fraudsters, or those under their control, will often become aggressive and threatening, even when asked to comply with entirely routine document or information checks to try and prevent you carrying out scrutiny.

Read more about reliance in the Legal Sector Affinity Group Anti-money Laundering Guidance, chapter 4.4.

4.3   Identify other solicitors or conveyancers

Fraudsters may pose as a solicitor or a conveyancer acting for either party to add greater legitimacy to the transaction. If you do not know them, you should check the recognised directory of their professional body.

- Find a Solicitor

- Directory of Licensed Conveyancers

You can also check a solicitor's details with the SRA over the telephone. Their contact number is 0370 606 2555.

Some fraudsters will try to assume the identity of professionals who actually exist. You should check that both the details and the final destination of documents match the details in the directory.

You may consider contacting the firm directly by the contact details on the registry if you have concerns about the bona fides of the representatives on the other side to the transaction, particularly if there is a last minute change of representative.

You should not transfer funds to the seller's solicitors without contacting their firm and checking the accuracy of the account details you have been supplied with.

Be aware that there have been occasions when professional directory information has been out of date or incorrect. Consider carrying out other reasonable checks including online free tools, or other paid-for services, to verify the legitimacy of the other professional.

4.4 Consider all information on the retainer

4.4.1 Sources of information

The following information may be relevant in assessing the risk of a retainer, in monitoring of the retainer, and in resolving concerns when mortgage fraud risks appear:

- documents involved in the retainer
- comments by the client in interviews
- correspondence or telephone conversations
- comments by other parties to the transaction or their representatives
- previous retainers for the client

4.4.2 Does it all add up?

You should consider whether the property and mortgage are consistent with what you know about the financial position and sources of income available to the client.

EXAMPLE:

You may have prepared a will for a client and done conveyancing on the purchase of a modest family home. If, a few years later, they then instruct you in the purchase of a holiday home that appears to be beyond their means according to earlier retainers, this would warrant closer inspection of the mortgage application. You should ask questions of the client to verify this information.

You should check all mortgage and contractual documentation carefully. Seek explanations from the client for any discrepancies in the document. It may be a simple misunderstanding of the documents or an inadvertent error needing correction.

You should consider whether the identity you have been given is consistent with the actual presentation of the client and the transaction as a whole.

4.4.3 Ensure documents are fully completed

You may receive contract documents that are not fully completed. For example, dates may be missing, the identities of parties not fully described, or financial details not fully stated. You should ensure all relevant sections of documents are completed before your client signs them, to avoid incorrect or fraudulent information being added later.

4.5 Signatures

You must ensure that you and your staff only witness signatures where you have actually seen the person signing the document. If any contract or mortgage documents have been pre-signed, you must either:

- verify it was pre-signed in the presence of a witness, or
- have the documents re-signed in your presence.

You should take note of all signatures on transaction documents and consider examining and comparing signatures with other available documentation if:

- you notice a discrepancy between signatures on the documentation
- you have concerns about the identity of any of the parties to the transaction
- the transaction is higher risk because it exhibits a number of the warning signs of mortgage fraud
- you notice that witness signatures appear to be those of a related party.

You may be asked to sign an independent legal advice certificate. Do not sign the certificate if you have not provided such advice.

4.6 Recording the property value

You should ascertain the true net cash price to be paid, to comply with the UK Finance Lenders' Handbook, BSA Mortgage Instructions, and Land Registry requirements. You should consider any direct payments, allowances, incentives or discount in ascertaining this price.

You should state this amount as the consideration in all of the following documents:

- contract
- transfer documents
- mortgage instructions
- certificate on title to the lender
- Land Registry forms

You should seek to understand any discrepancy between the value recorded in any of these documents, or if you are asked to enter a different value.

If you discover discrepancies in the valuation of the property between any of the relevant documents, you should consider your obligations to disclose this information to the lender.

In the event that a payment for chattels appears high, you should consider requiring an independent, professional valuation.

If you discover discrepancies in the valuation of the property between any of the relevant documents, you should consider your obligations to disclose this information to the lender.

Part one of the UK Finance Mortgage Lenders' Handbook and section C3 of the BSA mortgage instructions say you must report such changes to the lender. However, individual lenders may vary this obligation, either by using part two of the UK Finance Handbook, or through the specific instructions they provide.

Also consider your obligation to the lender to disclose any direct payments between the buyer and seller either already made, or proposed, that are not included in the mortgage instructions.

4.7 Changes to the retainer

You should stay alert to any changes in the circumstances of the retainer that may affect the agreed basis of the mortgage provision. These may include changes to the purchase price or previously undisclosed allowances, incentives or discounts.

Such arrangements may mean that the purchase price is different to that in the lender's instructions. In general, lenders will reasonably expect to receive such information, as it may affect their decision to grant the mortgage, or the terms of granting the mortgage.

You should ask questions to understand any changes. You should consult the lenders instructions, the UK Finance Handbook part two or the BSA mortgage instructions to assess your obligations to disclose this information to the lender.

4.8   Form LL and other restrictions

If a property owner wishes to safeguard against a fraudulent disposition of their property, they can apply for the entry of a Form LL restriction on the title.

Where the restriction is in place, no disposition of the property will be registered without a conveyancer's certificate, signed in their own name, that the conveyancer is satisfied that the person dispensing with the property is the same person as the proprietor.

A conveyancer's certificate will also usually be required where an application is made to withdraw or cancel a Form LL restriction.

If you are considering placing a Form LL or another restriction on the title, or are dealing with a property that is subject to this restriction, please read further information in HM Land Registry's guidance on notices and restrictions.

Be aware that placing a restriction on the title is in some cases equivalent to guaranteeing the identity of the registered proprietor. This may make lifting the restriction challenging in future, for example where the conveyancer retires.

5   CONFIDENTIALITY AND DISCLOSURE

5.1   SRA Handbook obligations

5.1.1   Chapter 3

You must not act for a buyer and a lender if a conflict of interest exists or arises between them. You have a conflict of interest if you have information about the conveyance that the lender would consider relevant to granting the loan, but the client does not want you to tell the lender.

5.1.2   Chapter 4

You must disclose relevant information to the lender client. Any change to the purchase price, or information reasonably expected to be important to the decision to grant the mortgage, will be relevant to the lender.

However this obligation of disclosure to the lender client is overridden by your duty of confidentiality to the purchaser client. This duty of confidentiality can only be waived with the consent of the purchaser client, or if it is required or permitted by law.

While you should always seek clarification from your client if you discover any discrepancies in relevant information, you may wish to streamline the consent process.

You may include a section in your standard terms and conditions for conveyancing clients, which provides that you will advise the lender client of any relevant information arising during the retainer. To rely on this approach for consent, you should:

- specifically bring this term to the client's attention at the outset of the retainer, and
- have them sign to signify acceptance of the terms and conditions.

5.2 When can you tell the lender?

Where you believe a purchaser client has provided incorrect or incomplete information to a lender during the mortgage process, you must seek consent from them to provide the correct information to the lender. If your purchaser client refuses, you must refuse to continue to act for them and the lender.

You must still consider legal professional privilege and your duty of confidentiality before passing information to the lender, even after you have ceased to act for a client.

You are only released from your duty of confidentiality where you are satisfied of a strong prima facie case that the client, or third party, was using you to further a fraud or other criminal purpose. This test may be satisfied if a client has made deliberate misrepresentations on their mortgage application.

If you are not released from the duty of confidentiality, you should simply return the mortgage documents to the lender and advise that you are ceasing to act due to professional reasons, without providing any further information.

For further advice on whether you need to cease to act in a matter and whether you can provide information to the lender, contact the SRA's Professional Ethics Helpline, or seek independent legal advice.

5.3 When can you tell law enforcement?

You must consider the money laundering risk if you discover or suspect that a mortgage has been obtained fraudulently, and the funds have been received by the client, either into their account, or your client account.

You must consider making a disclosure to the National Crime Agency (NCA). You must also consider your duty of confidentiality and legal professional privilege before you do so.

Importantly, making a disclosure to the NCA is merely a defence to money laundering offences. It is not a crime report. You may also make a report to your local police if you feel an investigation is warranted.

For further information on money laundering offences and making disclosures to the NCA, see the Legal Sector Affinity Group Anti-money Laundering Guidance.

For further information on whether legal professional privilege prevents you from making a disclosure to either the NCA or the lender you may take legal advice. You can find a list of solicitors offering such advice in the Law Society's AML directory.

For further advice on whether you need to cease to act in a matter, contact the SRA's Professional Ethics Helpline.

5.4 Alerting your insurer

Banks frequently try to recover mortgage fraud losses from professionals involved in conveyancing. If you suspect mortgage fraud has occurred, you should consider your obligations to your professional indemnity insurer.

For further information on possible civil liability, see the Legal Sector Affinity Group Anti-money Laundering Guidance, Chapter 11.

5.5 Tipping off

You may be concerned about tipping off offences under the Proceeds of Crime Act 2002, in talking to the lender, insurer, or your purchaser client.

A key element of these offences is the likelihood of prejudicing an investigation. The risk of this is small when disclosing to a reputable lender or your insurer. They are also regulated for the purposes of anti-money laundering and subject to the same obligations. There is also a specific defence of making a disclosure for the purposes of preventing a money laundering offence.

In relation to asking further questions of your client and discussing the implications of the Proceeds of Crime Act 2002, there is a specific defence for tipping off for legal advisers who are seeking to dissuade their client from engaging in a money laundering offence.

For further advice on tipping off, see Legal Sector Affinity Group Anti-money Laundering Guidance, Chapter 6.8.

For further information about avoiding tipping off in a particular case, contact the NCA's Financial Intelligence Helpdesk on 020 7238 8282.

6 MORE INFORMATION AND PRODUCTS

6.1 Legal and other requirements

Several pieces of legislation impose obligations on you with respect to property transactions. If these obligations are breached, criminal sanctions can follow.

- Fraud Act 2006
- Proceeds of Crime Act 2002 (as amended)
- Money Laundering, Terrorist Financing and Transfer of Funds (Information on the Payer) Regulations 2017

6.2 More information and products

6.2.1 Training and support

- Legal Sector Affinity Group Anti-money Laundering Guidance
- [UK Finance] Mortgage Lenders' Handbook – what's expected of you when working with lenders.
- Building Societies Association Mortgage Instructions
- Law Society Property Section – access the page for specialist advice and information

6.2.2 Law Society publications – available from our online bookshop

- *Anti-Money Laundering Toolkit*, 2nd edition
- *Conveyancing Handbook*, 22nd edition
- *Conveyancing Protocol*
- *Conveyancing Checklists*, 2nd edition
- *Conveyancing Forms and Procedures*, 4th edition

6.2.3 Practice Advice Service

The Law Society provides support for solicitors on a wide range of areas of practice. The Practice Advice Service can be contacted on 020 7320 5675 from 9am to 5pm on weekdays.

6.2.4 Professional Ethics Helpline

Contact the Solicitors Regulation Authority's Professional Ethics Helpline for advice on conduct issues.

6.2.5   Risk and Compliance Advisory Service

If you require further support, the Law Society's Risk and Compliance Advisory Service can help. We offer expert and confidential support and guidance, including face-to-face consultancy. Please contact us on 020 8049 3748, or email riskandcompliance@lawsociety.org.uk.

APPENDIX H2

Land Registry early completion practice note[1]

LEGAL STATUS

This practice note is the Law Society's view of good practice in this area. It is not legal advice.

Practice notes are issued by the Law Society for the use and benefit of its members. They represent the Law Society's view of good practice in a particular area. They are not intended to be the only standard of good practice that solicitors can follow. You are not required to follow them, but doing so will make it easier to account to oversight bodies for your actions.

Practice notes are not legal advice, nor do they necessarily provide a defence to complaints of misconduct or of inadequate professional service. While care has been taken to ensure that they are accurate, up to date and useful, the Law Society will not accept any legal liability in relation to them.

For queries or comments on this practice note contact the Law Society's Practice Advice Service.

PROFESSIONAL CONDUCT

The following sections of the Solicitors' Code of Conduct 2007 are relevant.

- Rule 1.01 Justice and the Rule of Law
- Rule 2 Client relations
- Rule 3 Conflict of interest
- Rule 3.07 Acting for lender and borrower in conveyancing transactions
- Rule 4.01 Duty of confidentiality
- Rule 4.02 Duty of disclosure
- Rule 10 Relations with third parties

SRA PRINCIPLES

There are ten mandatory principles which apply to all those the SRA regulates and to all aspects of practice. The principles can be found in the SRA Handbook.

The principles apply to solicitors or managers of authorised bodies who are practising from an office outside the UK. They also apply if you are a lawyer-controlled body practising from an office outside the UK.Terminology

---

[1] © The Law Society. This practice note is as stated on 9 July 2009. Practice notes are updated by the Law Society from time to time. Solicitors are advised to check **www.lawsociety.org.uk** for the latest version.

TERMINOLOGY

'**Completion'** – LR in the context of 'early completion' use this to mean acceleration of when they will make the first changes to the register in connection with the applications received.

'**You'** – The solicitor making the application to LR – the applicant's solicitor.

'**Charge'** – This may refer to more than one charge that is it includes first ,second and third charges.

'**Held over'** – The process whereby LR puts incomplete applications to one side pending receipt of the information necessary to complete the application

'**Registration Completion Sheet (RCS)'** – The new form that LR will use in place of the completion of registration letter that accompanies an application completed on the basis of early completion.

'**Title Information Document' (TID)** – This is issued by LR following completion of an application for registration with an official copy of the register. The TID explains why the official copies have been issued.

Must – A specific requirement in the Solicitor's Code of Conduct or legislation. You must comply, unless there specific exemptions or defences provided for in the code of conduct or relevant legislation.

Should – Good practice for most situations in the Law Society's view. If you do not follow this, you must be able to justify to oversight bodies why this is appropriate, either for your practice, or in the particular retainer.

May – A non-exhaustive list of options for meeting your obligations. Which option you choose is determined by the risk profile of the individual practice, client or retainer. You must be able to justify why this was an appropriate option to oversight bodies.

The Law Society also provides a full glossary of other terms used throughout this practice note.

1 INTRODUCTION

1.1 Who should read this practice note?

Solicitors dealing with conveyancing matters for buyers, sellers and lenders.

1.2 What is the issue?

From 3 August 2009, Land Registry (LR) will introduce 'early completion'. The early completion policy will apply to any situation involving a discharge of whole and another application. This new process relates to the procedure for, and the order in which LR will process multiple applications including discharge of a seller's charge.

Applications containing such multiple requests will be treated as separate applications. For example this means that where applications to discharge a seller's charge, transfer title to the buyer, then register the buyer's charge are made together, but evidence of discharge does not accompany the application and has not already been received by LR, LR will complete registration of the other applications, where possible.

This will leave the entries relating to existing charge(s) subsisting in the register. A transfer to a buyer and the buyer's charge might be registered before a seller's charge is removed from the title. Early completion may apply regardless of the method of discharge being used by the seller's lender.

Crucially, LR early completion does not mean legal or physical completion of the transaction. It simply means acceleration of when LR will make the first changes to the register in connection with the applications received. This practice note gives advice on:

- how early completion will operate
- handling applications where the registered proprietor's charge contains a restriction
- how to proceed with the different applications
- undertakings
- discharges
- identification
- fees.

2 THE ESTABLISHED PROCEDURE ON SALE

LR currently treat applications to discharge the seller's charge, transfer to the buyer and add the buyer's charge as linked and conditional upon each other. They are dealt with in that order.

So until evidence of discharge of the seller's charge is available to LR and has been registered, all of the applications are held over, except where the discharge takes place by ED or e-DS1.

LR allow applications like this to be held over several times, awaiting proof of satisfaction of a charge if you do all of the following:

- make a request for an extension of time
- keep LR informed as to progress
- show that you are actively pursuing the matter
- show that the lender is causing the delay.

LR consider requests for further extensions of time beyond an initial 20 business day period on their merits. Such extensions are granted largely when LR think it is realistic that the discharge will be produced in a reasonable time.

The applications to discharge, transfer and charge are likely to be cancelled, if:

- it appears unlikely that the discharge will be produced in a reasonable time
- you are not able to explain the reason for the delay or what is being done to obtain proof of satisfaction of the charge.

Provided that LR receive your application before 3 August 2009 it will be processed under the established procedure; LR will requisition for a discharge if this is not lodged before or with the application.

3 EARLY COMPLETION FROM 3 AUGUST 2009

Early completion will apply when you make an application to register (for example, for a sale remortgage or lease) that accompanies an application to discharge an existing charge of whole, and proof of satisfaction of that charge does not accompany or precede the application.

When you make an application like this, LR will reject the application for discharge, but will complete the other applications, where possible. The entries relating to the existing charge will be left on the register until LR receive proof of satisfaction of repayment of the mortgage.

How LR deal with the application will depend upon whether or not a restriction is registered in favour of the existing chargee.

3.1 Sellers' charges without restrictions

Early completion will operate immediately where the seller's charge does not contain matters on which requisitions need to be raised. The registrations will happen in the order that complete applications are received by LR, subject to the effect of any priority search. Complete applications are those that are ready to be processed with no documents missing or to follow.

If there are matters on which requisitions need to be raised LR will include a reminder about the missing discharge in their requisition but the missing discharge will not be a point on which a requisition is raised.

This may result in the transfer and the new charge being registered without the prior charge being removed.

3.2 Sellers' charges containing a restriction

When acting for a buyer, you should establish any relevant restrictions early in the transaction from the proprietorship register. This is prudent because the content of the restriction on the register will determine how LR will apply the new policy.

Restrictions in favour of a proprietor's chargees may prevent the registration of any further charge or in most cases of any disposition without the chargee's written consent. In such cases, the LR will requisition for either:

- proof of satisfaction of the charge
- evidence of compliance with the restriction.

If the lender does not provide evidence of the discharge within twenty business days, you will not be able to address the requisition within that time. In these circumstances, the LR will allow a further twenty business day extension if you do all of the following:

- make a written request for the extension
- demonstrate that you are actively pursuing the matter
- show that the existing lender is causing the delay.

LR has not given further formal guidance on these requirements. We assume that they will operate as before 3 August 2009 if you are unable to satisfy the requisition within the time limit.

LR will cancel both your application for discharge and applications to register the transfer and charge, where there is a restriction against the registration of any disposition. This time limit is up to forty business days if you have successfully applied for an extension. At the expiration of the time limit the application will be cancelled. LR will allow less time for satisfying any requisitions under early completion.

It may be of some benefit to make an additional priority search immediately prior to legal completion to extend the initial time available within which to obtain the evidence of discharge.

In the rarer case of a restriction only against the registration of charges, LR will complete the registration of the transfer, and cancel the application for discharge, which will leave the existing charge entries on the register. LR will also cancel the application for the new charge. The face of the register will then show the buyer as registered proprietor and the seller's lender as the mortgagee.

3.3 If your application is cancelled

As now, if your application is cancelled, you might lose priority for the application, unless you re-submit it within the priority period and it is subsequently registered.

Unless the further application is made within any existing priority period, priority for the interest will be lost if there is any competing application and/or search made before you made a further application to register the disposition, or received a further clear search. Making a further search will give you a new priority period, not extend the original one. The new search cannot act retrospectively and attach itself to the substantive application already lodged.

As is the case currently, the application will be subject to any other application or search made in respect of the property before your new search takes effect. If, for example, a further search is made at the time an extension is requested, whilst it will remain in the LR day list for thirty business days, it will not provide protection for the pending application. The application will have priority by virtue of it having been lodged at LR and entered in the day list. This means that from day thirty, when your search expires, to day 40, when your extension expires, the application will have priority by virtue of its entry in the day list and not by virtue of your search.

The new search may provide priority for any renewed application but this will depend on whether any other search and/or applications have been lodged before the search is received by LR.

Where there is a restriction and either early completion has been applied or LR has cancelled applications because of failure to satisfy a requisition, any official search protecting the cancelled application will remain in effect until its expiry.

3.4 Following the first part of the registration process

To avoid early completion leaving sellers' or outgoing charges on the register for a long time after completion of other parts of the registration, you should do both of the following:

1. Check the Registration Completion Sheet (RCS) letter you receive from LR to understand the status of the registration and to establish whether you should make further applications to conclude the necessary registration, particularly in relation to cancelling the seller's charge.
2. Establish office procedures to monitor the status of recently made and completed applications.

LR will make it very clear on the RCS where registration has been completed on the basis of early completion, and what other steps should be taken depending on the nature of the application. LR is currently developing the proposed wording.

3.5 The further application for registration of the discharge

3.5.1 Discharge by DS1

Where you are awaiting a paper DS1 you should make your subsequent application for registration of the discharge when you receive the DS1 from the seller's lender or seller's solicitor.

3.5.2 Discharge by Electronic Notification of Discharge (END)

ENDs do not incorporate an application to register, so you will need to establish if the END is available before making your second application in form AP1 or DS2E for the charge entries to be cancelled.

Lenders should notify the seller's solicitor, who will usually be redeeming the seller's charge, when they have sent an END to LR. The seller's solicitors in most cases will not be making application to redeem the seller's charge. You, the buyer's solicitor, will usually be making this application. This is why it is important that the sellers' solicitors immediately pass such information or notification as they receive from the lender to you. Some lenders, in relation to some electronic methods of discharge, provide no further notification following the redemption statement.

You can make a day list enquiry of LR to find out if an END transmitted by the lender is awaiting registration or view the register to find out whether the charge has been removed electronically.

Alternatively you can phone the relevant local LR office to establish that:

- the charge entries have been cancelled following receipt of an ED or e-DS1
- an END, ED or e-DS1 has been received, or
- no END, ED or e-DS1 has been received.

This is a free service.

You can also contact LR telephone services centre to make an END enquiry. Call 0844 892 0307 for properties in England and 0844 892 0308 for properties in Wales and for the Welsh speaking service.

3.5.3   Restrictions against the registration of charges

In the case of a restriction against the registration of charges rather than against any disposition, LR will register the transfer and then requisition as set out in 3.2 above. If LR then receive the discharge LR will register this and subsequently register the buyer's charge which will be part of the application they are already holding provided that time limits have not been exceeded and the application has not been cancelled. This applies to discharges by both DS1 and END.

3.5.4   Discharge by ED and E-DS1

Both of these kinds of electronic discharge incorporate an application to LR to discharge the charge. You therefore do not need to make any further application to LR to register the discharge but to comply with your obligations you do need to monitor the status of the original application.

3.6   Title Information Documents (TIDs)

A TID will be issued as usual following completion of a registration. LR will issue the RCS and the TID which includes an official copy of the register.

LR will issue a TID and an official copy of the register after the subsequent application.

LR are considering the following issues:

- whether and how notification should be sent to you when a charge left on the register after early completion is subsequently discharged by an ED or a e-DS1.
- whether any such notification should also include an updated official copy of the register.

3.7   Lenders' checking of the register

Lenders are likely to continue to make checks to establish when applications for registrations have been made following a purchase and whether they were they made within the priority period. Once early completion is introduced, lenders are likely to want to know whether they have a registered first charge and whether any former charges have been removed from the register. The fact that lenders may be carrying out these checks does not relieve you of your duty to the lender to make your own checks.

4   COUNCIL OF MORTGAGE LENDERS (CML) HANDBOOK

The CML Handbook states that on completion of the instructions in a retainer, the lender will require a fully enforceable first legal charge. The CML say this requirement remains unchanged by LR's early completion processes. The CML's view is that early completion is not an issue substantially affecting the current process. Accordingly they do not propose to amend the Handbook.

The CML states:

> The order of events may in some cases be reversed but the stages of the process remain exactly the same.
>
> Lenders regard completion as having taken place once the retainer is complied with. It is not relevant that the Land Registry has imposed an intervening stage in the transaction as this does not change the overall position.

By 'completion', the CML means completion of the instructions from a lender, not legal or physical completion.

In connection with the CML Handbook LR states that:

> Completing the applications to register the transfer and new charge subject to the existing charge would not appear to affect the obligations of any party in relation to that existing charge. If the existing charge has been repaid then the requirement on the lender to provide evidence of proof of satisfaction of that charge will remain. The obligation of the seller's conveyancer arising from any undertaking given to the buyer's conveyancer in relation to the charge will not change.
>
> Early completion will not prevent the new charge taking effect as a first legal charge; it can never become a first charge until the existing charge is discharged. This is so whether or not the new charge is entered in the register. The entry of the new charge under early completion simply protects the priority of that new charge as against any other interest whose priority is not protected at the time of registration.

The CML states that the changes will not alter the requirements set out in paragraph 14.1.1.1 of the CML Lenders Handbook which require the conveyancer to register the mortgage as a first legal charge at the Land Registry. Lenders do not regard the retainer as being complied with until this is achieved.

By implication this suggests that lenders will not regard the temporary situation, of the buyer's mortgagee having a second mortgage whilst the seller's mortgage is awaiting discharge, as being in breach of the provisions of the CML Handbook. This is so because lenders will not regard completion as having taken place until the retainer has been completed by the lender being registered with a first legal charge. It is upon completion of, and not during, the retainer, that lenders require a first legal charge.

5   UNDERTAKINGS AND ASSURANCES

Early completion is a policy change that does not directly affect the existing advice in the *Conveyancing Handbook* and Rule 10 of the Code of Conduct in relation to undertakings.

The changes in practice arising from early completion may make you, as a buyer's solicitor, want to seek further assurances from the seller's solicitor. You may seek these by way of representations, contractual obligations and/or undertakings.

Where you seek a further or extended undertaking to meet the requirements of the early completion policy, the seller's solicitor will need to consider whether any such extended undertaking can properly be given. It may not be possible, or proper for the seller's solicitor to give such extended undertaking.

In order to attempt to meet the requirements of early completion you may instead seek pre-contract representations or warranties from the seller's solicitors that they will:

- pay over the money required to discharge the charge on completion
- press the lender for the discharge
- endeavour to obtain from the lender and will supply to the buyer information about the likely method of discharge to be used

- in the absence of DS1, DS3 or END notices continue to press for such information and supply such information as is available to them as to the status and likely issue time of the release.

Note carefully that a 'representation' or 'warranty' to do something could well amount to an undertaking (see Solicitors' Code of Conduct rule 10.05 and the associated guidance).

These assurances may assist in providing you with the necessary information to enable you to apply to the LR for extensions of time or to make further priority searches. However, even if the seller's solicitor provides full information this will not resolve the problem. If the discharge is not available within the extended time limits the application is likely to be rejected, but the information you receive may assist you in assessing the risk of this occurring in any transaction.

Making a further priority search does not guarantee protection. Making a further search will give you a new priority period; it will not extend the original one. The search result will be subject to any other application or search made in respect of the property before your new search takes effect. In these circumstances you will be acting in your clients' interest by requesting and obtaining such assurances from the seller's solicitor to ensure that priority for the buyer's registration of ownership and the lenders registration of charge is protected.

Solicitors acting for sellers can reasonably be expected to co-operate in affording such information and assurances as are reasonable as this will, in most cases, be in their own clients 'best interests.'

For further information on conveyancing undertakings to discharge mortgages see both:

1. rule 10.05 of the Solicitors' Code of Conduct
2. the *Conveyancing Handbook*, 19th edition. The relevant sections are section E.3, F.4 and the guidance on accepting undertakings after *Patel* v. *Daybells* [2001] EWCA Civ 1229 in appendix IV.7.

See also the SRA warning card on undertakings updated in April 2009.

This provides that 'you must ensure that your undertakings are specific, measurable, agreed, realistic and timed.'

6 DISCHARGES

Lenders may use any of a variety of methods available to them for effecting a discharge. This brings uncertainty because the nature of the form of discharge used affects the timing of the availability of the discharge for registration.

The discharge may be evidenced by a DS1, an ED, an END or an e-DS1.

A buyer's solicitor may attempt to establish from the seller's solicitor the nature of the discharge that will be used in the transaction. However this is unlikely to provide certainty as to the method that will ultimately be used.

The reasons for this are:

- The seller's solicitor may not know the form of discharge that the seller's lender is proposing to use until quite a late stage in the transaction.
- The nature of discharge may change during the course of a transaction. For example, some electronic methods of discharge revert to paper if they cannot be processed electronically for some reason.

In addition, some lenders:

- operate different methods of discharge for different members within the same group
- use multiple methods of discharge that change according to the nature of the mortgage product.

Nonetheless as set out in paragraph 4 above it may assist you to request from the seller's solicitor information about the likely method of discharge to be used. It is factor that may help you to assess the risks.

From 27 July 2009, LR will make available an updated version of their Practice Guide – 31: Discharges of Charges.

7 IDENTIFICATION REQUIREMENTS (ID)

When making the second application to register the paper discharge of the seller's discharge you will not need to provide a new ID form if LR has retained form ID1 or ID2 in respect of the lender for a charge being discharged by a paper DS1. This is so long as the evidence of identity is no more than three months old at the time the further application is made after early completion.

You should add a note to panel 13 of form AP1 to refer LR to the ID form you have already provided.

This is only relevant where the solicitor is not representing the discharging lender. This should already have been established in replies to TA13 Completion arrangements and requisitions, if not earlier.

You may make provision in the contract for when evidence of identity becomes more than three months old, because it will be difficult to establish, in advance, cases in which evidence is likely to be or may be more than three months old. You can provide that such provisions do not merge on completion. See Standard Conditions of Sale (4th edition) condition 7.4.

This also applies to evidence of identity for the borrower or lender for a new charge in respect of which the LR has cancelled an application.

8 APPLICATION OF EARLY COMPLETION

8.1 Transfers of Part

LR will not complete applications to register transfers of part on the basis of early completion but say they will keep the position under review. LR will requisition for a discharge of part if one is required and not lodged with an application to register a transfer of part. However LR will continue to operate the process as now without implementing early completion.

8.2 Charges of Part

Early completion does not apply to applications that only comprise an application for a discharge of part of a charge to be registered.

8.3 Remortgages

Early completion presents fewer concerns when applied to remortgages where the borrower in relation to the incoming and outgoing charges will be the same, as there will be no undertaking between sellers and buyers solicitors. However the status of the application needs to be monitored to ensure that the new lender obtains a first legal charge.

8.4 Leases

LR states that it already applies a form of early completion when dealing with applications to register a dispositionary first lease where there is a charge registered against the landlord's title. Although the charge is not usually discharged when a lease is granted, the absence of the chargee's consent to the grant of a lease by the landlord does not prevent the lease from being registered with absolute title.

In relation to the transfer or assignment of leases subject to a mortgage, rather than the grant of a lease, early completion will apply as at 3 above.

8.5   Discharges

Where the application to remove the registered charge is the only application made, and the evidence is not available to LR when the application is received LR will reject it as being substantially defective under rule 16(3) of the Land Registration Rules 2003, regardless of the method of discharge. This is because the new early completion procedures relate to applications to remove the entries relating to a registered charge where evidence of discharge is not supplied with, or prior to, the application. This is the only circumstance in which the LR will reject, rather than cancel an application.

See the following for further information:

- LR PG 50 Requisition and cancellation procedures
- LR PG 49 Return and rejection of applications for registration

9   FEES

9.1   LR fees

No further fee is payable if you need to make a further application to remove the charge entries that remain after early completion. This remains true if your further application also includes the registration of a new charge rejected under early completion, provided that you lodge a copy of the Registration Completion Sheet (RCS) sent following completion of your original application.

9.2   Your fees

When estimating your charges at the start of the retainer, you may wish to give advance notice of any additional work that you may have to carry out as a result of early completion. These may include likely additional LR fees, additional priority search fees and/or lodgement of restriction fees in addition to your professional charges as the operation of this policy is likely to involve you in spending additional time on each matter.

10   MORE INFORMATION

10.1   Legal and other requirements

- Land Registration Amendment Rules 2008 (as amended) (LRR)
- Land Registration Act 2002 (as amended) (LRA) various but see sections 16, 27(2)(a) and (f)
- Land Registration Rules 2003 (as amended) (LRR) various but see rule 114 and 115
- Fraud Act 2006
- Money Laundering Regulations 2007
- Proceeds of Crime Act 2002 (as amended)
- CML Handbook

10.2   Further products and support

10.2.1   Practice Advice Line

The Law Society provides support for solicitors on a wide range of areas of practice. Practice Advice can be contacted on 020 7320 5675 from 09:00 to 17:00 on weekdays.

10.2.2   Other practice notes and Law Society materials

- Mortgage fraud [practice note]
- Anti-money laundering [practice note]
- Property Section
- Land Registry Identity requirements
- Membership benefit: First Title

10.2.3 Law Society publications

- Land Registry Practice Bulletin 16 Early Completion (PDF)
- Land Registry Early Completion FAQs
- Conveyancing Handbook [25th edition]
- Conveyancing Protocol
- Conveyancing Checklists [3rd edition]

10.2.4   Council of Mortgage Lenders

The CML is the trade association for the mortgage lending industry and represents first charge lenders. Not all lenders are members of the CML.

- CML handbook
- CML FAQs

10.3   Acknowledgements

- Law Society Conveyancing and Land Law Committee
- Law Society E-Conveyancing Task Force
- Law Society Property Section

Property and registration fraud practice note[1]

LEGAL STATUS

This practice note is the Law Society's view of good practice in this area. It is not legal advice.

Practice notes are issued by the Law Society for the use and benefit of its members. They represent the Law Society's view of good practice in a particular area. They are not intended to be the only standard of good practice that solicitors can follow. You are not required to follow them, but doing so will make it easier to account to oversight bodies for your actions.

Practice notes are not legal advice, nor do they necessarily provide a defence to complaints of misconduct or of inadequate professional service. While care has been taken to ensure that they are accurate, up to date and useful, the Law Society will not accept any legal liability in relation to them.

For queries or comments on this practice note contact the Law Society's Practice Advice Service.

PROFESSIONAL CONDUCT

The following sections of the Solicitors' Code of Conduct 2007 are relevant to this issue:

- Rule 1.01 Justice and the Rule of Law
- Rule 2 Client relations
- Rule 3 Conflict of interest
- Rule 3 Acting for lender and borrower in conveyancing transactions
- Rule 4.01 Duty of confidentiality
- Rule 4.02 Duty of disclosure

SRA PRINCIPLES

There are ten mandatory principles which apply to all those the SRA regulates and to all aspects of practice. The principles can be found in the SRA Handbook.

The principles apply to solicitors or managers of authorised bodies who are practising from an office outside the UK. They also apply if you are a lawyer-controlled body practising from an office outside the UK.

TERMINOLOGY

The register – The register of title, except in the context of cautions against first registration (s.132 LRA 2002)

---

[1]   The Law Society. This practice note is as stated on 11 October 2010. Practice notes are updated by the Law Society from time to time. Solicitors are advised to check **www.lawsociety.org.uk** for the latest version.

Conveyancer – A solicitor, a licensed conveyancer within the meaning of s.11(2), Administration of Justice Act 1985, a Fellow of the Institute of Legal Executives (r217(c), LRR 2003), a barrister (r217(d), LRR 2003), a duly certificated notary public (r217(e), LRR 2003), or a registered European lawyer (r217(e), LRR 2003)
Legitimate owner – The rightful claimant to the land or the interest in land whose rights require protection, which could include someone with the right to apply for first registration; a registered proprietor; a registered proprietor of a charge; or someone with the benefit of an interest such as a notice or restriction See LRA 2002 for definitions
Property – Any land or interest capable of registration under LRA 2002
Criminal property – Property that:

(a) constitutes a person's benefit from criminal conduct or it represents such a benefit (in whole or part and whether directly or indirectly), and
(b) the alleged offender knows or suspects that it constitutes or represents such a benefit (Section 340(3) of the Proceeds of Crime Act 2002)

Organised crime – Two or more people involved in continuing significant illegal activities; such a group is capable of defending its members with violence, coercion or corruption; and more than £1m in criminal proceeds has been generated
Law enforcement agencies –

(a) the Commissioners or any other government department
(b) the Scottish Administration
(c) any other person who is charged with the duty of investigating offences or charging offenders, or
(d) any other person who is engaged outside the United Kingdom in the carrying on of activities similar to any carried on by the NCA or a police force

(Section 3(4) (a) of the Serious Organised Crime and Police Act 2005)

Must – A specific requirement in the Solicitor's Code of Conduct or legislation. You must comply, unless there specific exemptions or defences provided for in the code of conduct or relevant legislation
Should – Good practice for most situations in the Law Society's view. If you do not follow this, you must be able to justify to oversight bodies why this is appropriate, either for your practice, or in the particular retainer
May – A non-exhaustive list of options for meeting your obligations. Which option you choose is determined by the risk profile of the individual practice, client or retainer. You must be able to justify why this was an appropriate option to oversight bodies

The Law Society also provides a full glossary of other terms used throughout this practice note.

1   INTRODUCTION

1.1   Who should read this practice note?

All solicitors who carry out work involving Land Registry applications.

1.2   What is the issue?

Fraud is on the increase and there is a rising incidence or awareness of fraudsters targeting the properties of both individuals and companies. These attacks often include identity and other types of fraud and the presentation of forged documents to Land Registry for registration. Land Registry wishes to bring these matters to the attention of the public and have issued public guides to this effect.

This practice note aims to assist you when acting in property transactions. It may also help you make your clients more aware of how they may protect their property interests against fraud and safeguard their rights as legitimate property owners on the register.

This advice is not exhaustive. Many aspects of mortgage fraud can also be adapted to commit registration fraud. For further information see the Law Society practice note on mortgage fraud.

2 FRAUD THREATS FOR PROPERTY TRANSACTIONS

2.1 Impersonation of conveyancers and conveyancing practices

Those proposing to carry out fraud may purport to:

● be a conveyancer in their own right, or
● work for an authorised practice.

If you do not know either the conveyancer or the conveyancing practice acting for another party in a matter you should check their details to help assess the risk of fraud.

When accepting identification (or any other) information from a person holding themselves out to be a conveyancer you should consider the following:

● Is the individual a conveyancer?
● Is the name of the signatory an identifiable registered individual within a conveyancing practice?
● Are they registered with an appropriate professional body?

The Law Society, the Solicitors Regulation Authority (SRA), the Council for Licensed Conveyers (CLC), The Institute for Legal Executives (ILEX) and other professional bodies hold such information [...]. More information is provided in the Conveyancing Handbook under 'Dealing with non-solicitors'.

Where a party is unrepresented and you are unable to confirm that sufficient steps have been taken to verify that party's identity, Land Registry requires you to provide certified identification information obtained by you or another conveyancer in respect of that party. This is explained in Land Registry's Practice Guide 67 – *Evidence of identity – conveyancers* with specimen forms.

Obtaining identification information at an early stage in the transaction may avoid difficulties or delays at a later stage. You may wish to keep a record of the steps you take. These may assist you if Land Registry or other bodies contact you to make enquiries but see [...] below on reporting fraud.

2.1.1 Impersonation of solicitors' firms

There have been instances where fraudulent applications have been made to Land Registry by fraudsters impersonating legitimate firms of solicitors by using forged headed paper, faxes and emails. Email addresses that are non distinct, for example hotmail addresses, are more difficult to trace.

If you receive communications from Land Registry, including any acknowledgement of an application, and you are unable to identify the client name, the property or the application reference you should contact Land Registry. It is possible that your firm name or its headed paper has been forged or misappropriated and used fraudulently by a third party, or even a member of your staff.

See [...] below on reporting fraud.

2.1.2   Misuse of websites

Web sites have been fraudulently set up purporting to be sites of solicitors and/or new sub-offices of legitimate firms in order to perpetrate fraud. Some firms periodically search the internet to establish if they are being targeted in this way. If you become aware of an unauthorised web presence for your practice you should notify the relevant agencies.

2.2   Seller and buyer frauds

Certain properties and owners are particularly susceptible to fraud. Most fraudulent activity falls into distinct categories:

- Intra-family/associate frauds which are perpetrated by family members, friends or partners.
- Third party frauds where tenants or those who have access to tenants and are able to divert post perpetrate the fraud.
- Third party frauds that constitute 'organised crime'.

2.2.1   Contact details

Client contact details may suggest an increased risk of fraud, such as:

- where the only contact details provided for any party are a telephone number, mobile number and/or an email address
- where a family member or associate is gifting the property and you are instructed by and meet only one party to the transaction, and only have contact with the other party by post, telephone or email
- where the address is not the subject of the transaction without obvious reason
- where the address changes occur mid-transaction without obvious reason.

There may be entirely valid reasons for all of these examples.

2.2.2   Vulnerable registered owners

Land Registry has identified that certain categories of owners may be more susceptible to registration frauds. These vulnerable registered owners include, for example, elderly owners who are in hospital or have moved into a care home. These types of owners often own properties without a legal charge. Attempts could be made to sell or charge their property by use of identity fraud.

Owners who live abroad are also particularly vulnerable to this type of fraud.

Some clients may be particularly at risk from fraudulent activity because, for example:

- they no longer live in the property and there was an acrimonious break up with a partner
- they let the property or it is empty
- they have already been the victim of identity fraud
- they are a personal representative responsible for a property where the owner has died and the property is to be sold.

2.3   Vulnerable properties

Land Registry has identified that certain types of properties may be particularly vulnerable to registration frauds, such as:

- unoccupied properties, whether residential or commercial
- tenanted properties
- high value properties without a legal charge

- high value properties with a legal charge in favour of an individual living overseas
- properties undergoing redevelopment.

2.4 Keeping addresses up to date

In order to minimise risk where there are vulnerable registered owners or vulnerable properties Land Registry advises registered proprietors to keep any addresses they have registered for service at Land Registry up to date. See Land Registry *Public Guide 2 – Keeping your address for service up to date.*

Clients intending to leave their property empty for a significant period of time, such as, for redevelopment purposes, should consider registering some other address(es) for service. (see paragraph 4.2.1).

3 MITIGATING FRAUD THREATS

3.1 Client identity

You should be aware that exercising reasonable care in viewing documents intended to establish identity may not conclusively prove that the person or company is the person or company they are purporting to be. In addition it may not be possible for you to conclusively establish that such person or company is either the registered proprietor of the relevant property or entitled to become so registered.

Even where you have followed usual professional practice the court may hold that the steps taken exposed someone to a foreseeable and avoidable risk and amounted to a breach of duty of care. See *Edward Wong Finance Co Ltd* v. *Johnson Stokes & Master* [1984] 1 AC 296.

3.1.1 *Conveyancing anti-money laundering*

Conveyancing transactions are regulated activity under the Money Laundering Regulations 2007. You must therefore take steps to:

- identify and verify your client by independent means
- identify and, on a risk-sensitive approach, verify any beneficial owners, and
- obtain information on the purpose and intended nature of the business relationship.

This last requirement means more than just finding out that they want to sell a property. It also encompasses looking at all of the information in the retainer and assessing whether it is consistent with a lawful transaction. This may include considering whether the client is actually the owner of the property they want to sell.

You should also comply with Money Laundering Regulations and Law Society general practice information.

For further information about fraud prevention see the Law Society's anti-money laundering practice note.

You may keep a record of any steps you take.

3.1.2 *Address for service at Land Registry*

Since July 2008 Land Registry has inserted an entry in the register indicating whether the registered proprietor has changed their address for service (see paragraphs 4.2 and 4.2.1 below), to alert people to the change. For example, the entry may state: 'The proprietor's address for service has been changed'. People proposing to commit fraud have been known to change the address for service registered at Land Registry as a precursor to fraud. If you see this on your client's register and are not aware of the reason for it you may ask your client why it was done.

3.2 Surrounding circumstances

Further factors you may consider include the following:

- Where the registered proprietor is a company, does a search at Companies House indicate that the company was incorporated after the registered proprietor was registered as the owner?
- Have you met your client face to face?
- Have you seen the original identity documents or only copies?
- Is the registered proprietor's date of birth inconsistent with their being the owner?

For example:

Someone purports to be a registered proprietor and offers identification information, but there is an inconsistency between their date of birth and information on the register.

The date appearing immediately before a proprietor's name in the proprietorship register is the date of registration of that owner:

(13.10.1970) JOHN SMITH and JANE SMITH

In this example the proprietors have been registered since 1970 and must have been at least 18 at that time. Consequently, if, in cases where you are seeing the client face to face, the person presenting the identification information appears too young, this may be a case of impersonation.

3.3 Company impersonation

If the company was incorporated after the registered proprietor was registered as the owner the registered proprietor is unlikely to be the legitimate owner. Despite appearing to have the same company name, the discrepancy of dates will indicate dealing with a company of the same name but not necessarily the 'real' registered proprietor. You should note that an Industrial and Provident Society that has converted into a company registered under the Companies Acts would be an exception to this situation.

One notable registration fraud involved the impersonation of an overseas company by the setting up of a UK company with the same name. If a search at Companies House states that the date of incorporation of the UK company is after the date of registration of the property in that company's name, further enquiry should be made.

The date of registration [as proprietor] is the date appearing in brackets immediately before the company name in the proprietorship register. A discrepancy without any legitimate reason may be a risk factor.

3.3.1 Foreign companies

Since January 1999 Land Registry has been entering the company's/corporation's country of incorporation in the proprietorship entry. In some cases this will also include the state or province of incorporation, for example incorporated in Delaware, USA. This information appears in the register immediately after the corporation's name.

If an overseas company has a registration number issued by Companies House because it has a branch or place of business in the UK, that registration number is also included in the proprietorship entry as follows:

Proprietor:- NORDDEUTSCHE LANDESBANK GIROZENTRALE (incorporated in Germany) (UK Regn. No. FC012190) of ....

If there is no Companies House registration number this may help you identify a registered proprietor as an overseas company, provided it was registered after January 1999. If the registered proprietor is a foreign company, a UK company with the same name is unlikely to be able to give instructions as the registered proprietor of the property.

Verification of the identity of an overseas company may require confirmation from a qualified lawyer authorised in the country of incorporation. See Land Registry Practice Guide 67 – *Evidence of identity: conveyancers*.

3.3.2 Searching Companies House

Where no place of incorporation and no UK company number are noted on the register, you may be able to establish the date of incorporation by making a search of Companies House. The results of searches of Companies House may assist in assessing the risk of an overseas company impersonation.

3.4 Identity document provisions

You should be aware of the provisions relating to identity documents in the following documents:

- AML requirements
- [UK Finance Mortgage] Lenders' Handbook
- BSA instructions

3.5 Enhanced due diligence

Where you do not see a client face-to-face, the Money Laundering Regulations 2007 provide that you must undertake enhanced due diligence. Not undertaking face-to-face checks may increase the risk of the transaction being exposed to investigation by the law enforcement agencies and/or the SRA.

For further information see paragraph 4.9.1 of the Law Society's anti-money laundering practice note.

Non face-to-face transactions increase the risk of fraud and these risks may be mitigated in the following ways.

- If you are accepting instructions from one client on behalf of others or by a third party, rule 2.01(c) of the Code of Conduct requires you to check that all clients agree with the instructions given . For example, an unwary conveyancer might deal solely with the son or daughter of a registered proprietor and have no contact with the person who is the owner.
- Where you know or have reasonable grounds for believing that your instructions are affected by duress or undue influence, you should bear in mind also the provisions of rule 2.01(d).
- In the case of a third party charge created to secure debts of another, you should consider contacting the purported lender independently. If there is a purported representative for the lender, then consider contacting that representative for confirmation of the transaction. In these circumstances there is a regulatory requirement for separate representation.

Risks of fraud are increased if documents are provided to clients for execution other than in the presence of you or your staff.

In order to protect or to mitigate risk for you and your firm, you may keep a contemporaneous record of the steps you take, including the reasons why you took a particular decision and the consideration you gave to risk.

4 LAND REGISTRY REQUIREMENTS

4.1 Freedom of Information (FoI) 2000

Wherever possible Land Registry tries to assist law enforcement agencies and regulatory bodies with the prevention and detection of fraudulent activity. It is bound by the provisions of the FoI 2000, which embodies a general principle of transparency in relation to the disclosure of information within government departments. This means that requests for information, which may relate to your particular application or the conduct of your account with Land Registry, may be received from third parties.

Following an FoI request, if Land Registry has reason to believe disclosure of the information would, or would be likely to, prejudice the prevention or detection of crime, or the administration of justice, then under the provisions of s.31 FoI 2000, Land Registry will consider whether the issue of such information is in the public interest. If Land Registry considers such disclosure is not in the public interest the request may be refused under s.2(2)(b) FoI 2000.

If a person is dissatisfied with a refusal of a FoI 2000 request, an application can be made to the Information Commissioner for a decision under s.50 FoI 2000.

Where Land Registry considers such a disclosure to be in the public interest it will supply the information requested to the law enforcement agency or other body or person requesting it.

4.2 Notices and addresses for service

Clients need to ensure their address for service is always up to date and can be directed to Land Registry for further information. The following Land Registry public guides are available.

- *Public Guide 2 – Keeping your address for service up to date*
- *Public Guide 17 – How to safeguard against property fraud*

Where appropriate, Land Registry may require further documents or evidence, or may give any necessary or desirable notice under r.17 Land Registration Rules (LRR) 2003 (as amended) as a means of verifying information about certain transactions. This enables Land Registry to stop processing an application while further enquiries are made or law enforcement agencies notified where necessary.

If the proprietor's address for service is out of date they will not receive any such notice from Land Registry and will increase their exposure to fraudulent activity.

Some clients are more at risk than others, such as:

- buyers who will not be living at the property purchased may register multiple addresses for service. These may include those who live abroad, and landlords of commercial and residential property
- recent buyers who are moving from a property they still own may need to maintain an up-to-date address for service in relation to that property.

4.2.1 Addresses for service

Clients may use more than one address for service in the register. There must be at least one postal address, including an overseas address, and each registered proprietor can register up to three addresses (r.198 LRR 2003) in total.

The inclusion of additional addresses for service can give added protection to a legitimate owner as:

- the address of the property the client is selling may not be an effective address for service
- the address of the property the client is buying may not be the address where the client is contactable.

Additional addresses may be:

- another property address
- an email address, or
- the address of a professional adviser (such as a DX address).

The address of a professional adviser is most suitable for use where there is an ongoing relationship, such as, an accountant providing continuing tax advice.

You should not give the address of your firm as an address for service unless you are confident that you will be able to contact your client immediately should you receive notification from Land Registry. You should be aware that such notice may not be received for many years following the conclusion of a matter and if you have acted only, for example, in the purchase of a property, you are unlikely to know whether the client has moved or sold and whether you hold up-to-date contact details for them.

Land Registry notices usually require a response within 15 days. If the address for service is outside the jurisdiction, Land Registry has no discretion to extend this time. An email address may ensure Land Registry communications reach clients even when they are away from their properties, or where post is at risk of interception.

4.3 Indemnity

Schedule 8 of the Land Registration Act (LRA) 2002 (as amended) provides for the payment of indemnity for loss suffered by reason of (among other things) the rectification of the register and certain mistakes in the register.

Under Schedule 8, paragraph 5(1) (b), no indemnity is payable if the loss is wholly as a result of the claimant's lack of proper care. Under Schedule 8, paragraph 5(2), any indemnity will be reduced if the loss is partly as a result of the claimant's lack of proper care.

Land Registry may seek to limit its indemnity in certain circumstances where it considers that the conveyancer failed to make reasonable checks in relation to identity.

There is case law which establishes that a lack of proper care by a conveyancer will be attributable to their client, and may therefore lead to a reduction in any indemnity payable to the client. An example of a case in which delayed notification by a conveyancer to Land Registry led to such a reduction is *Prestige Properties Ltd* v. *Scottish Provident Institution and another* [2002] EWHC 330 (Ch).

5 REPORTING FRAUD

5.1 Professional requirements

Rule 4 of the Solicitors' Code of Conduct deals with confidentiality and disclosure and your obligations when considering whether disclosure to a third party is necessary or appropriate. In particular Rule 4.01 sets out the fundamental duty that the affairs of your client(s) and former client(s) must be kept confidential except where disclosure is required or permitted by law or by the client/former client.

The SRA Guidance (see notes 9 to 19) to Rule 4 describes the exceptional circumstances when disclosure of confidential information is required or permitted; for example, where statute requires disclosure to specific government or other bodies, or in order to comply with Proceeds of Crime Act (POCA) 2002 and Money Laundering Regulations 2007, or where the solicitor's conduct is under investigation by the SRA or the Solicitors Disciplinary Tribunal.

5.1.1   Disclosure

Where disclosure may be permitted or required by law, you must ensure that you understand the scope of your obligation in the absence of the client's specific consent, ie by considering the relevant provisions of the statutory power, and whether privileged information is protected from disclosure. You should only provide such information as you are strictly required by law to disclose.

Disclosure of confidential information which is unauthorised by your client or by the law could lead to disciplinary proceedings against you and could render you liable to a civil action by your client arising out of the misuse of confidential information.

5.1.2   Duty of confidentiality

The duty of confidentiality is not applicable if the retainer with the client is tainted by fraud. Confidentiality does not apply to information acquired by a solicitor where they are being used by a client to facilitate the commission of a crime or fraud, because that is not within the scope of a professional retainer. You should judge the likelihood of such an occurrence in the light of your client's explanations and any other relevant factors.

5.1.3   Other considerations

The other conduct and legal issues which you will need to consider in relation to this section are the following.

- Rule 1 – core duties.
- Rule 2.01 – taking on and ceasing to act for clients.
- Rule 5.01 – supervision and management responsibilities.
- Rule 20 – rights and obligations of practice.
- Legal professional privilege.

In April 2009 the SRA issued property fraud and money laundering warning cards for solicitors to help you when assessing risk.

You should therefore consider notifying Land Registry if you identify a registration fraud. If you are acting for a victim of fraud or someone you believe is a victim of fraud you should consider notifying Land Registry at the earliest opportunity subject to the other obligations set out in this paragraph 5.

If, after careful consideration of your professional obligations, you have evidence that you or someone else has been a victim of a fraud or that someone is attempting to commit a fraud, you may also decide that it is in the public interest to report that fraud. […]

5.2   Money laundering and disclosure to the National Crime Agency (NCA)

If you know or suspect that a fraud has been committed and a person is in possession of criminal property, you must consider the provisions of Proceeds of Crime Act (POCA) 2002.

The person in possession of the criminal property does not have to be your client, and you do not actually have to be involved in the transaction. In those circumstances you must still consider section 332 of POCA 2002 and whether you need to make a disclosure to the NCA to avoid committing an offence.

A disclosure to the NCA is only a defence to money laundering offences; it is not a crime report. You may need to make a separate report about the fraud to law enforcement agencies. See the Law Society's anti-money laundering practice note.

You should consider implications regarding the offence of 'tipping off' under POCA 2002 if you have included information about the making of a SAR in reporting the fraud to law enforcement agencies.

While the provision of this information to such bodies is not required by law, a key element of the offence of tipping off is the likelihood of prejudicing an investigation. This risk is small when disclosing to law enforcement agencies, or to an appropriate person at the Land Registry. There is also a specific defence of making a disclosure for the purposes of preventing a money laundering offence. [...]

6   CIVIL LIABILITY

6.1   Land Registry's rights of recourse

Land Registry has statutory rights to recover money it has paid out by way of indemnity. Under Schedule 8, paragraphs 10(1)(b) and (2)(a) of LRA 2002 it is entitled to enforce any right of action which a person to whom it has paid indemnity would have had if that person had not been indemnified.

Similarly, under Schedule 8, paragraphs 10(1)(b) and (2)(b), it is entitled to enforce any rights of action which a person in whose favour the register has been rectified would have been entitled to enforce if the register had not been rectified. The registrar may have a right of recourse against a conveyancer under either head. However, Land Registry's policy is that it does not seek recovery from a conveyancer who has not been at fault, even though there may be circumstances where, strictly, it would have a right to do so.

6.2   Contractual liability

You should consider whether you have complied with the terms of your retainer and other professional obligations. For example, have you given any undertakings to obtain the signature of a particular person? You should also consider if you have given any warranty to a party to the transaction (other than your client) that you have the authority to act for a person in the transaction. Case law illustrates the circumstances in which the liability for breach of warranty can create an absolute liability or one actionable only on proof of negligence. See the following cases.

- *Penn* v. *Bristol & West Building Society and others* [1997] 3 All ER 47.
- *Zwebner* v. *The Mortgage Corporation* [1998] PNLR 769.
- *Midland Bank* v. *Cox McQueen* [1999] 1 Lloyds Rep PN 223.
- *Halifax Plc* v. *Espley and others*. QBD (Leeds). 23 May 2000 (Unreported).

7   MORE INFORMATION

7.1   Legal and other requirements

- Land Registration Rules 2008 (as amended)
- Land Registration Act 2002 (as amended)
- Land Registration Rules 2003 (as amended)
- Fraud Act 2006
- Money Laundering Regulations 2007
- Proceeds of Crime Act 2002 (as amended)
- [UK Finance Mortgage] Lenders' Handbook

7.2   Products and services

7.2.1   Law Society publications

- *Conveyancing Protocol*

- *Conveyancing Checklists*
- *Solicitors and Money Laundering: A Compliance Handbook*
- *Conveyancing Handbook ...*
- The Law Society mortgage fraud practice note
- [Anti-money laundering guidance for the legal sector]
- SRA property fraud warning card
- SRA money laundering warning card

7.2.2 Land Registry guides

- Practice Guide 67 – *Evidence of identity: conveyancers*
- Public Guide 2 – *Keeping your address for service up-to-date*
- Public Guide 17 – *How to safeguard against property fraud*
- Public Guide 20 – *Evidence of identity: non-conveyancers*

7.2.3 Practice Advice line

The Law Society provides support for solicitors on a wide range of areas of practice. Practice Advice can be contacted on 020 7320 5675 from 9am to 5pm on weekdays.

7.2.4 Land Registry enquiries

For queries relating to Land Registry please contact Land Registry on 0844 892 1111.

7.3.5 Professional bodies

- The Law Society
- Solicitors Regulation Authority
- Council for Licensed Conveyancers
- Institute of Legal Executives

7.3 Acknowledgements

The Law Society and Land Registry have worked in close collaboration on the production of this practice note.

Price and service transparency practice note[1]

From 6 December 2018, firms will be required to publish information about certain price, service and regulatory matters.

This practice note offers support to solicitors in deciding how to comply with these new requirements.

LEGAL STATUS

This practice note is the Law Society's view of good practice in this area. It is not legal advice.

Practice notes are issued by the Law Society for the use and benefit of its members. They represent the Law Society's view of good practice in a particular area. They are not intended to be the only standard of good practice that solicitors can follow. You are not required to follow them, but doing so will make it easier to account to oversight bodies for your actions.

Practice notes are not legal advice, nor do they necessarily provide a defence to complaints of misconduct or of inadequate professional service. While care has been taken to ensure that they are accurate, up to date and useful, the Law Society will not accept any legal liability in relation to them.

For queries and comments on this practice note, contact the Law Society's Practice Advice Service.

PROFESSIONAL CONDUCT

The following sections of the SRA Code of Conduct 2011 are relevant for this issue:

- Outcome 1.12
- Outcome 1.13
- Outcome 1.9
- Outcome 1.10
- Outcome 8.1
- Outcome 8.2
- Indicative behaviours 1.13-1.21
- Indicative behaviour 8.7
- Indicative behaviour 8.8
- Indicative behaviour 8.9

This practice note will be updated if the SRA Code is replaced by two new Codes (which currently await approval from the Legal Services Board).

---

[1]   © The Law Society. This practice note is as stated on 1 November 2018. Practice notes are updated by the Law Society from time to time. Solicitors are advised to check **www.lawsociety. org.uk** for the latest version.

SRA PRINCIPLES

There are 10 mandatory principles that apply to all those the SRA regulates and to all aspects of practice.[1] The principles can be found in the SRA Handbook.

In publicising price and service information, you should consider:

- Principle 2 – act with integrity
- Principle 4 – act in the best interests of each client
- Principle 5 – provide a proper standard of service to your clients
- Principle 6 – behave in a way that maintains the trust the public places in you and in the provision of legal services
- Principle 7 – comply with your legal and regulatory obligations and deal with your regulators and ombudsmen in an open, timely and co-operative manner

The SRA has also issued non-mandatory ethics guidance giving its views on ways in which firms might comply with the Transparency Rules.

TERMINOLOGY

- **Must** – A specific requirement in legislation or of a principle, rule, outcome or other mandatory provision in the SRA Handbook. You must comply, unless there are specific exemptions or defences provided for in relevant legislation or the SRA Handbook.
- **Should** – Outside of a regulatory context, good practice for most situations in the Law Society's view. In the case of the SRA Handbook, an indicative behaviour or other non-mandatory provision (such as may be set out in notes or guidance).

  These may not be the only means of complying with legislative or regulatory requirements and there may be situations where the suggested route is not the best possible route to meet the needs of your client. However, if you do not follow the suggested route, you should be able to justify to oversight bodies why the alternative approach you have taken is appropriate, either for your practice or in the particular retainer.
- **May** – An non-exhaustive list of options for meeting your obligations or running your practice. Which option you choose is determined by the profile of the individual practice, client or retainer. You may be required to justify why this was an appropriate option to oversight bodies.
- **SRA Code** – SRA Code of Conduct 2011
- **O** – Outcome
- **IB** – Indicative behaviour

1 INTRODUCTION

1.1 Who should read this?

This should be read by all solicitors, and in particular those who are involved in providing services to individual and small businesses. The new SRA Transparency Rules will come into force on 6 December 2018 and price information must be published for a limited number of services specified in the Rules.

The display of an SRA digital badge[2] will also be required. It is expected that the digital badge will be made available for firms to use from December 2018. Display of the digital badge will not be mandatory until 2019.

1.2 What is the issue?

The SRA has published its Transparency Rules that require all authorised firms and sole practitioners to publish price and service information on their websites, or to provide it to prospective clients on request if a firm does not have a website, for specific legal services.

The requirements aim to ensure that accurate and relevant information about a solicitor or firm is made available at the pre-engagement stage. The services which are caught by the Rules tend to be those accessed more by individuals and small businesses, but you should review the affected services carefully.

The intention is that the public will be able to use this information to make more informed choices, improving transparency and competition in the legal market. The price publication requirements apply to all firms who publish as part of their normal business that they provide relevant services. The requirements apply even where a firm specialises in providing relevant services to more affluent individuals or large business clients.

The focus is on providing further information on firms' websites. As well as being an important marketing and promotion tool for you and your firm, your website will most likely be a significant gateway to your firm for consumers.[3] Perceptions and judgements about a firm and its services are formed within seconds of viewing a website. Law Society research[4] shows that legal services consumers may search a number of websites to understand likely providers and offerings.

The Rules[5] do not require your firm to have a website. However, if you do not have a website, you are required to ensure that the same information is available for clients on request – for example, in a brochure or leaflet.

Our research and other sources suggest that consumers make their decisions based on a range of factors including reputation, price, convenience and speed. You may therefore consider whether you wish to provide additional information beyond the minimum required in order to attract prospective clients.

2 GENERAL OBLIGATIONS

The SRA Transparency Rules require the publication of certain information on websites and there are SRA Code obligations that underlie these new requirements:

- you must ensure your publicity is accurate and not misleading (O 8.1)
- you must ensure clients are in a position to make informed decisions about the services they need, how their matter will be handled, and the options available to them (O 1.12)

Not all information will need to be provided at the pre-engagement stage.

3 MEDIUM OR FORMAT

Rule 1.1[5] requires an authorised firm or sole practitioner to publish cost information on its website. While the Rules refer to 'cost' information this is to be understood from a consumer's perspective: i.e. it is a requirement to publish the price of your service.

This rule does not require you to acquire a website if you do not already have one. Acquiring a website remains a commercial decision for you or your firm to make.

If you do not have a website, you must ensure that the required information (except for the digital badge) is available on request (Rule 3.1). This should allow a client to obtain the information without the need for a formal consultation or formal engagement. You could create leaflets or brochures for clients to pick up from offices, or you could hold the information so that it can be emailed or posted to a client on request.

The remainder of this practice note focuses on publishing information on a website, but many of the principles will be applicable to firms without websites who must provide information on request.

4   REGULATORY AND COMPLAINT INFORMATION

All firms and sole practitioners must now publish information regarding their regulatory status and their complaints procedure for clients.

4.1   Complaints procedure

You must publish details of your complaints handling procedure on your website, including how and when a complaint can be made to the Legal Ombudsman and to the SRA (Rule 2.1).

You are already required to inform clients in writing at the time of engagement about the right to complain, how complaints can be made and when a client can make a complaint to the Legal Ombudsman (O 1.9-1.10). You must also have a procedure for handling complaints (see IB 1.22 for the elements highlighted by the SRA Code).

You may choose to use or adapt some of the information in your client care letters to meet this new requirement to publish information. For more information on handling complaints please refer to our practice note on handling complaints.

The SRA intends to issue standard wording on how to refer complaints to the Legal Ombudsman and the SRA.

4.2   Regulatory information

If you are an authorised body, you must display in a prominent place on your website your SRA number and the SRA's digital badge. It is expected that the digital badge will be made available for firms to use from December 2018. Display of the digital badge will not be mandatory until 2019. The SRA has indicated that it will provide guidance for firms to help in setting up the badge correctly.

Rule 4.2 requires that your letterhead and emails show your SRA authorisation number and the words 'authorised and regulated by the Solicitors Regulation Authority'. The SRA Code already requires you to do this (O 8.5). For more information on this please refer to our practice note on information on letterheads, emails and websites.

5   COST INFORMATION

In addition to the above, you must publish cost information for certain services if you are a firm or sole practitioner who 'publishes as part of its usual business the availability of any of the [specified] services'. Publicly funded work is excluded from this requirement.

5.1   Areas of practice

Rules 1.3 and 1.4 list the services for which cost information is required, divided into services for individual and business customers respectively.

The services in relation to individuals are (Rule 1.3):

- **Residential conveyancing:** The conveyance of residential real property or real estate which comprise: (i) freehold or leasehold sales or purchases; or (ii) mortgages or re-mortgages.[6]
- **Administration of an estate:** The collection and distribution of money, property and other assets belonging to a person following their death, where these are within the UK and the matters are not contested.[7]
- **Immigration:** The preparation and submission of immigration applications (excluding asylum applications); and the provision of advice and representation at the First-tier Tribunal (Immigration and Asylum Chamber) in relation to appeals against Home Office visa or immigration decisions, excluding asylum appeals.[8]

- **Motoring offences:** The provision of advice and representation at the Magistrates Court in relation to summary only road traffic offences dealt with at a single hearing.[9]
- **Employment Tribunal:** The provision of advice and representation to employees in relation to the bringing of claims before the Employment Tribunal against an employer for unfair dismissal or wrongful dismissal.

The services in relation to businesses are (Rule 1.4):

- **Employment Tribunal:** The provision of advice and representation to employers in relation to defending claims before the Employment Tribunal brought by an employee for unfair dismissal or wrongful dismissal.
- **Debt recovery:** Debt recovery up to the value of £100,000.
- **Licensing applications:** The provision of advice and assistance and representation in relation to licensing applications for business premises.[10]

5.2 Publishing the availability of services

You must publish price information if you publish, as part of your usual business, the availability of any services listed in Rules 1.3 and 1.4.

The SRA Handbook Glossary 2012 defines publicity widely to include all promotional material and activity, including the name or description of your firm, stationery, advertisements, brochures, websites, directory entries, media appearances, promotional press releases, and direct approaches to potential clients and other persons, whether conducted in person, in writing, or in electronic form, but does not include press releases prepared on behalf of a client.

In addition, online material and social media postings emanating from or on behalf of your firm/organisation are likely to be considered publicity. If any of this promotional material suggests that one or more of the specified services is offered by you or your firm as part of its usual business, you will need to ensure your website includes price information in accordance with the Rules.

There are certain instances where the publication requirements will not apply. If you do not publish that you offer the specified services but agree to carry out work in one of the specified areas for an existing or new client, you will not (for that matter) become subject to the price publication requirements.

5.3 General obligations

There are general obligations you must comply with regarding price and service information contained in the SRA Code:

- your publicity must not be misleading or inaccurate (O 8.1)
- charges should be clearly expressed and state whether VAT or disbursements are included (O 8.2)
- avoid estimating charges at unrealistically low levels (IB 8.7)
- do not describe normal overheads as disbursements (IB 8.8)
- do not advertise estimates/fixed feeds without making clear additional charges might apply (if that is the case) (IB 8.9)

You must publish cost information in a clear and accessible way, and in a prominent place on your website (Rule 1.6).

5.4   Price information

5.4.1   Costs and basis for charges

The Transparency Rules aim to ensure that the consumer has sufficient information providing a good indication of the likely costs prior to engagement with your firm and any retainer. You must include the total price of the service or, where not practicable, the average cost or range of costs including VAT (Rule 1.5(a)).

You must also include the basis for your charges, including any hourly rates or fixed fees (Rules 1.5(b)). The basis of your charges should be made as clear as possible – whether you use hourly rates, fixed fees or conditional fee agreements.

The Rules give some flexibility in how firms publish prices. If you are publishing average costs, it should be clear that the prices shown are estimates for a standard case, and that a full case specific estimate can be obtained by contacting you.

If publishing a range of costs, you should ensure that the range still provides consumers with a good indication of price based on your experience of previous cases.

If publishing a fixed fee, you should be clear about what the price includes and excludes. In general, you should ensure that any figures you publish are supported by an analysis of similar cases you have undertaken previously.

Where you set out a price for your service, you should set parameters on the nature of the problem you are advising on in that scenario. For example, if you publish information on conveyancing services, you could state that you are providing illustrative estimates relating to a freehold sale of a property at a price of approximately £300,000 and with specified assumptions. This will help a client to judge how your services may be priced in relation to their own matter.

You should also list factors that could increase overall costs. For example, factors that could affect the cost of a conveyancing matter include if the legal title is defective or part of the property is unregistered, if building regulations or planning permission has not been obtained or if there is a delay in receiving key documents.

If you choose to use an automatic quote generator then the generator must produce a quote directly without requiring any additional contact to be made. Your online quote generator should also be compliant with data protection legislation.

Unless you are charging a fixed fee, there is a reasonable chance that the average price you state on your website will not be the precise price that you end up charging every client. In order to avoid misunderstandings, you should consider making this clear alongside any price information that you publish.

5.4.2   How many different prices should you publish for each practice area?

For each practice area which you work in, you will need to decide how many different prices to publish on your website. For some practice areas the minimum requirement is clearer than others.

For probate work the Rules state that you must publish your price in respect of 'the collection and distribution of money, property and other assets belonging to a person following their death, where these are within the UK and the matters are not contested'. Therefore, for probate it appears that the minimum requirement is to publish a price for one clear standard case, although you must still decide whether to publish a fixed fee, a range of costs or an average cost.

For conveyancing, firms should publish price information for residential sales, purchases and mortgages or re-mortgages. If you choose to publish information for a freehold sale or purchase, you should note how the price will be different if it is a leasehold sale or purchase.

At the other end of the spectrum is immigration work. The SRA Rules state that you must publish cost information with regard to the following services:

- the preparation and submission of immigration applications, excluding asylum applications
- the provision of advice and representation at the First-tier Tribunal (Immigration and Asylum Chamber) in relation to appeals against Home Office visa or immigration decisions, excluding asylum appeals

In relation to immigration matters, the SRA's guidance breaks down the types of immigration work further by specifying that the following types of applications are covered by the Rules:

- applications for naturalisation or registration under the British Nationality Act 1981
- applications on behalf of European Economic Area (EEA) nationals and their family members under the applicable EEA Regulations or Immigration Rules, including applications for permanent residence, residence cards, and registration certificates
- applications under the Immigration Rules, including: student and work experience visas; visit visas (for tourism, or visiting friends / family); spouse and partners applications; including fiancé(e)s or proposed civil partners, applications for work, business or study under the Points-Based System; dependent relative and family reunion applications; ancestry visas; other categories, such as applications on the basis of long residence

The SRA guidance states that you are not required to publish prices for the following types of applications:

- asylum applications
- statelessness applications
- human rights/private life applications
- applications for Secretary of State immigration bail
- reconsideration and legacy requests
- judicial review, such as claims for unlawful detention
- immigration services to businesses (e.g. applications for certificates of sponsorship or confirmation of acceptance for studies)

The SRA guidance provides further information than the Rules in defining the range of immigration cases that you should publish prices for. Our understanding is that the Rules set out the minimum requirements, and it is the Rules which must be followed by all affected firms.

In deciding how many prices you will publish for different types of immigration work, you should ensure that anyone who looks at the prices you publish on your website can get as good an understanding as possible on the price of their own matter.

Publishing information on the basis of your charges (which you are required to do under Rule 1.5(b)) and noting factors that may increase or decrease prices (such as whether particular types of applications are likely to take more time) will help with this.

5.4.3   Publicising free, discounted and pro bono work

The Rules do not require you to specify any preferential rates which you may offer. You are also not prohibited from charging a lower rate than is published on your website.

If you publicise services as being 'free', you must only do so if they are not chargeable, rather than being linked to, or conditional upon, other factors such as receiving further instructions or other benefits.

If you publicise work as being carried out on a pro bono basis there must be no charges billed to the client, except where a conditional fee agreement is used and the only charges billed are those which your firm receives by way of costs from the client's opponent or other third party, and which are paid to a charity under a fee sharing agreement. If under a conditional fee agreement or damages-based agreement any costs would be recovered from damages or other compensation awarded to the client, this fact must be publicised.

5.4.4 Disbursements and VAT

You must include a description, and the cost, of any likely disbursements (Rule 1.5(d)). If the actual cost of a disbursement is not known, then you must list the average cost or range of costs (Rule 1.5(d)).

The term disbursements may not be well understood by clients and may require explanation, for example by describing a disbursement as 'costs payable to another organisation which are incurred by you as agency for your client'.

Your firm's overheads should not be described as disbursements and should not be included as additional charges that are passed on to your clients. Examples of overheads that should not be charged as disbursements include:

- annual subscription costs and transaction fees for using online solutions to manage business processes. This would not preclude such costs being passed on to clients, for example through an administration charge (as opposed to being described as a disbursement)
- petty charges such as postage, photocopying and faxes, and
- professional indemnity insurance.

You must also make it clear whether any fees or disbursements attract VAT and, if so, the amount of VAT they attract (Rule 1.5(e)).

5.4.5 Referral fees

Where your client has been referred as part of an arrangement with a third party who introduces business to you and/or with whom you share your fees (where permitted by the SRA Code), you must ensure that your client is informed of any financial or other interest which an introducer has in referring the client to you and of any fee sharing arrangement relevant to their matter (O 9.4 and 9.5).

This should include drawing clients' attention (in writing or in a form appropriate to the client's needs) to any payment or other consideration you make in connection with a referral (IBs 9.5 and 9.6).

Likewise if your client has been introduced to a third party you must account to the client for any financial benefit (any commission, discount or rebate) or other interest that you have in making that referral.

5.4.6 Conditional fee or damages-based agreements

If you use conditional fee or damages-based agreements, you must outline the circumstances in which clients may have to make payments themselves for your services, including from any damages (Rule 1.5(g)). If you want to assess the viability of a case before taking it, you should clarify how long you will spend doing that assessment.

5.5 Service-related information

You must detail what services are included in the price displayed, including key stages of the matter and likely timescales for each stage, and details of any services that might reasonably be expected to be included in the price displayed but are not (Rule 1.5(f)).

Some firms offer free initial interviews for clients, while others include interviews at cost. You should state whether an initial client interview is included.

Clients are unlikely to have a clear understanding of the stages of handling a legal matter or the technical aspects of a case. Jargon should be avoided and steps should be explained, for example, 'preparation of an ET1' in an employment tribunal case may require further explanation for consumers.

You may wish to consider laying out the stages of a matter along with the services you provide at each stage. When outlining the timing for a matter you may wish to link to information on other websites, for example visa processing times on the Home Office website.

You should also set out the assumptions you make as to the nature of the matter. For example, if you set out a leasehold conveyancing matter you may say that you assume that landlord management information is not delayed in being sent to you.

Publishing details of any services not included in the price is relevant to cases where there is unbundling of legal services. For example, if you offer unbundled services for immigration matters you should make it clear what the client takes responsibility for and what you take responsibility for (for example the client may take responsibility for initially completing their immigration form while you may be responsible for thoroughly reviewing, and making any changes to, the form).

Practitioners should give careful consideration to the appropriateness of unbundling in relation to the complexity of the case, the client's needs and their ability to benefit from unbundled services, and how best to present price information on that service accordingly.

For more information on unbundling, please refer to our practice note on unbundling civil legal services.

5.5.1 *Experience and qualifications*

You must include information on the experience and qualifications of anyone carrying out the work, and of their supervisors (Rule 1.5(c)). This rule does not require you to name a specific person who will work on the matter.

Instead, it is sufficient to provide general experience and qualification information on staff who work in the relevant team. It is expected that you will provide information on anyone carrying out fee earning work.

You may wish to provide a brief overview of your team, for example:

'Our conveyancing team is made up of Chartered Legal Executives (with 1-3 years' experience) and qualified solicitors (with at least 4 years' experience). The team is supervised by [partner name] who has over 15 years' experience working in residential conveyancing and qualified as a solicitor in 2002.'

If you already have a biographies section on your website that provides team information, then you do not need to include experience and qualifications information on the same page as the price information.

6 IMPLEMENTATION

You should consider the following points to help your firm comply with the new minimum requirements.

6.1 Your website capabilities

You may need to review the suitability of your firm's website provider. Information which you are required to publish could require updating or changing on a regular basis as prices becomes out of date, particularly if you are publishing detailed hourly rates or the cost of disbursements change (such as court fees).

Some website providers and administrators will allow changes to be made by you or your firm directly, and some may not. You will need to ensure that you have the capabilities to change information as necessary.

It may be helpful to time stamp information and note how regularly the information is reviewed. You may wish to assign someone with responsibility for conducting regular reviews to ensure your pricing information is up to date.

6.2 Clear, accessible and prominent

You must publish price information in a clear and accessible way, and in a prominent place on your website (Rule 1.6).

People have different understandings and perceptions about the legal market and may also behave in different ways as to how they receive information. You should therefore consider your target market, and tailor your information where possible to what consumers know.

For example, the Law Society's consumer behaviour research found that conveyancing clients are more likely to value speed of service delivery than other clients, while wills clients show a preference for expertise and experience over other areas.[11]

The following may assist with making your information more readable to clients:

- Online content should be kept as brief as possible. A range of research has shown that people read information online in a different way than on paper. People often don't read everything on a webpage, and instead skim read and their gaze is drawn to certain items (the top left corner of the page receives the most attention).
- You should use short sentences no more than two or three lines long, and brief, informative headings to guide the reader to important information.[12]
- Use simple, plain language where you can and avoid jargon if possible. For example, use 'try' instead of 'endeavour', or use 'other costs payable to another organisation' instead of 'disbursements'.[13]
- When searching for information, we often try to find it in the easiest, simplest and quickest way possible. Cost information should be put as 'close' to your homepage as possible, meaning no more than two clicks away. This reduces the effort needed to find it and helps make it more prominent.
- If you want to keep the content on your webpages as minimal as possible you could attach a PDF that provides price and service information, as long as the PDF is easy to access and in a prominent place on your website.

6.3 Client care information

Many firms use a client care letter to provide information to clients on price, service and complaints information. You may be able to use this information as a basis upon which you can develop your website information.

However, when you come to engage with a client then it is important to be clear what the terms of engagement are. Some clients will engage your services without having visited, or thoroughly engaged with the content on, your website.

Terms of service should therefore be provided to clients in addition to any information on your website. To avoid future complaints you should take care that there is no basis for confusion (see section 7 below).

6.4 Additional information

The new Rules are minimum requirements. You are therefore free to publish further information on your website if you wish to do so. This may help to demonstrate the value that consumers get from using your firm and your experience and expertise across relevant practice areas. This could help to differentiate yourself from competitors.

Examples of additional information you could publish include:

- customer reviews or testimonials
- case studies
- membership of accreditation schemes
- membership of professional bodies
- if you are ranked in the legal directories or have won awards
- relevant industry publications

7 ADVISING YOUR CLIENT ON THE BASIS OF COST INFORMATION

When a client subsequently seeks to engage your services, you are required to give your client the best possible information (both at the time of engagement and as their matter progresses) about the likely overall cost of their matter (O 1.13).

In particular you should take account of IBs 1.13-1.21, which indicate that you should:

- discuss whether the potential outcomes of the client's matter are likely to justify the expense or risk involved, including any risk of having to pay someone else's legal fees
- clearly explain your fees and if and when they are likely to change
- warn about any other payments for which the client may be responsible
- discuss how the client will pay, including whether public funding may be available, whether the client has insurance that might cover the fees, and whether the fees may be paid by someone else such as a trade union
- where you are acting for a client under a fee arrangement governed by statute, such as a conditional fee agreement, give the client all relevant information relating to that arrangement
- where you are acting for a publicly funded client, explain how their publicly funded status affects the costs
- provide the information in a clear and accessible form which is appropriate to the needs and circumstances of the client
- where you receive a financial benefit as a result of acting for a client, either pay it to the client, offset it against your fees, or keep it only where you can justify keeping it and the client has agreed to the amount
- ensure that disbursements included in your bill reflect the actual amount spent or to be spent on behalf of the client
- inform your client of incremental costs throughout your work and any changes to cost estimates

8 FEEDBACK

This practice note is designed to support solicitors in complying with the new Transparency Rules. The Law Society previously opposed these changes on the basis that regulation was not necessary or proportionate.

We highlighted the concerns we had about the additional burden of these changes, both in cost and capacity for many firms. We remain concerned about the impact on members and as such are committed to supporting you as much as we can to help you manage and respond to these changes.

We are interested in hearing about your experiences with the implementation of the new Rules, both positive and negative. This will help the Law Society to develop more useful and relevant guidance for members, and understand the impact of the new Rules for any future review by the SRA or the Law Society.

Case studies of your experiences or other feedback can be sent to: **regulation@lawsociety.org.uk**.

NOTES

1   The SRA Overseas Rules 2013 apply to regulated individuals practising overseas and to responsible authorised bodies.
2   The digital badge is a new initiative proposed by the SRA that SRA-regulated firms will need to display on their website. It will show that the firm is regulated by the SRA and is intended to act as a hyperlink to further information about consumer protection, to help the public understand who is SRA-regulated and the protections that come with it.
3   For more information, please refer to our practice note on protecting your online reputation.
4   View the Law Society's research [**www.lawsociety.org.uk/policy-campaigns/consultation-responses/sra-consultation-looking-to-the-future-better-information-more-choice-law-society-response**].
5   References to the Rules in this practice note are to the SRA Transparency Rules 2018 unless stated otherwise.
6   Transfers of equity (e.g. in divorce proceedings where the property is transferred from joint names into one of the parties' name as part of the financial settlement) is not covered by the Transparency Rules.
7   This includes both testate and intestate and taxable and non-taxable estates.
8   Please refer to section 5.4.2 'How many different prices should you publish for each practice area?' for further information on the types of immigration applications covered by the Transparency Rules.
9   Under Part I of the Road Traffic Act 1988 and s.89 of the Road Traffic Regulation Act 1984.
10   The Rules are limited to two types of applications – applications for a premises licence under s.17 of the Licensing Act 2003 and applications to vary a premises licence under s.34 of the Licensing Act 2003.
11   View a copy of the research [**www.lawsociety.org.uk/policy-campaigns/consultation-responses/sra-consultation-looking-to-the-future-better-information-more-choice-law-society-response**].
12   See also the Law Society blog on writing clearly and writing for digital audiences.
13   See the Plain English Campaign.

Accepting undertakings on completion following the Court of Appeal decision in Patel v. Daybells[1]

Accepting undertakings on completion

The first instance decision in *Patel* v. *Daybells* [2000] All ER(D) 1004 caused consternation among conveyancers. It held that it was negligent for a buyer's solicitor to accept an undertaking for Form 53 (now DS1), save in exceptional circumstances. The Court of Appeal ([2001] EWCA Civ 1229) has now upheld the decision that the solicitor in the case was not negligent, but reversed the reasoning – the acceptance of a solicitor's undertaking for a DS1 will not normally be negligent. But does this mean a return to business as usual?

The Court of Appeal held that 'conformity to a common (or even universal) professional practice is not an automatic defence against liability; the practice must be demonstrably reasonable and responsible'. This involves considering the risks involved and how to avoid them. The Court of Appeal was satisfied that the legal profession had considered the risks of accepting an undertaking and that in the standard case it was reasonable to rely on the existence of compulsory insurance, the Compensation Fund and the summary procedure for enforcing undertakings when assessing the extent of that risk. Other relevant factors were: the Council of Mortgage Lenders' advice to its members to discharge a mortgage even where insufficient funds were sent, if this was due to the lender's error; and the problems which would ensue if the buyer's solicitor had to communicate directly with the seller's lender.

Exceptional cases

The 'exceptional circumstances' in which it might be negligent for a buyer's solicitor to accept an undertaking were not specified by the Court of Appeal, although the court made it clear that the fact that the seller's solicitor was a sole practitioner did not make the transaction exceptional.

The court referred in detail to the expert evidence on behalf of the buyer's solicitor that it would not be normal or advisable to rely on an undertaking in two situations, but did not expressly endorse these as the relevant 'exceptional circumstances'. The two situations mentioned are:

---

[1] © The Law Society. Prepared by the Law Society's Conveyancing and Land Law Committee in May 2002.

- Where the amount required to redeem the seller's mortgage exceeds the minimum level of solicitors' indemnity insurance (currently [£2m] per claim); or
- Where the mortgagee is not a member of the Council of Mortgage Lenders.

Minimising the risks in exceptional cases

The risk of accepting an undertaking for a DS1 is that it might not be forthcoming (e.g. because of the fraud or negligence of the seller's solicitor or because of problems in identifying the amount required to redeem the mortgage). Default by the seller's solicitor is dealt with by the requirement for compulsory insurance and, ultimately, the Compensation Fund. Only where the figures exceed the compulsory level of insurance might the buyer's solicitor need to take additional steps to deal with that risk. The risk of a dispute with the lender should not normally be a problem where the lender is a member of the CML. Even disputes not covered by the CML's advice may not put the buyer's solicitor at risk: the Law Society's recommended form of undertaking puts an absolute obligation on the seller's solicitor to discharge the relevant mortgage. It is therefore the seller's solicitor who is at risk if the DS1 is not forthcoming: his obligations can be summarily enforced and are backed by compulsory insurance and in certain cases, the Compensation Fund.

In each of the exceptional cases mentioned in *Patel* v. *Daybells* the matter comes back to the safeguards put in place by the profession. The only variable is the level of insurance cover and that is only relevant in the case of large mortgages. Normally the buyer's solicitor does not know the amount of the debt (and the Court of Appeal disapproved of the idea that the buyer's solicitor should have to make such enquiries). It is common to ask in preliminary enquiries for confirmation that the sale price exceeds the amount secured on the mortgage. Provided the sale price is not more than [£2m], such confirmation should give the buyer's solicitor the necessary comfort to accept an undertaking from the seller's solicitor. In larger transactions the buyer's solicitor may wish to take additional steps before or instead of accepting an undertaking.

- The buyer's solicitor could ask the seller's solicitor to get express written confirmation from the lender that he has been appointed the lender's agent for the receipt of the redemption money. This places the risk of default or dispute with the lender and avoids the buyer having to investigate either the details of the mortgage or the seller's solicitor's insurance.
- The buyer's solicitor could insist on sending the redemption money direct to the lender. The buyer's solicitor should ask to see the redemption statement as independent evidence of the figure. The Court of Appeal disapproved of the buyer making such enquiries in the standard case but in an exceptional case, where large sums are involved, this may be inevitable. As this information is confidential to the seller, the seller's solicitor should get instructions before revealing it. However, this solution does not deal with the problem of a dispute over the amount required to redeem. It may also be difficult to arrange in the case of an 'all moneys' mortgage. If this course is followed, Standard Condition 6.7 should be amended (or, if using the Standard Commercial Property Conditions, expand condition 6.7). In either case, the issue must be addressed before exchange (or if using the Standard Commercial Property Conditions, expand condition 8.7).
- Where the amount of the mortgage debt exceeds the minimum indemnity insurance (as will often be the case in commercial transactions), a buyer's solicitor might only accept an undertaking for DS1 if coupled with a warranty from the seller's solicitor that his insurance cover exceeds the amount required to redeem the mortgage.
- Finally, there is no obligation to accept an undertaking in place of performance of the obligation. Indeed, solicitors have often been unwilling to accept an undertaking for the

192

DS1 in the case of a mortgage to a non-institutional or overseas lender or in the case of a private loan. However, if that is the buyer's solicitor's position, a contract condition that the DS1 must be available on completion will be necessary. In many cases this will not be a realistic option as institutional lenders' procedures do not include issuing the DS1 in escrow.

Before the buyer's solicitor accepts an undertaking where the expert evidence in *Patel* v. *Daybells* stated it would not be normal practice to do so, it is essential to explain the risks to the buyer and get clear instructions that the buyer is willing to take them.

Even where the lender is separately represented, the buyer's solicitor should consider whether there are any exceptional circumstances making it unwise (or potentially negligent) to accept an undertaking (or at least without evidence of the lender's solicitor's authority to accept the redemption money).

ENDs

The use of Electronic Notifications of Discharge (END) presents a particular problem as there is never a paper DS1 to be handed over: the buyer's solicitor is always reliant on an undertaking by the seller's solicitor to forward the redemption money and the END form to the lender, who then sends the discharge notification directly to the Land Registry. Even where the transaction might fall into the category of exceptional cases the buyer's solicitor will ultimately have no choice but to accept the undertaking and will have to take such steps as are available (e.g. split payments, evidence of the seller's solicitor's authority, evidence of sufficient insurance cover).

APPENDIX 12

Conflicts of interest – flowcharts[1]

These flowcharts are an easy reference guide to the outcomes and IBs on acting for buyer and seller and lender and borrower, which are outlined in chapter 3 of the SRA Code of Conduct 2011.

---

[1]   © The Law Society. Issued 14 February 2012.

BUYER AND SELLER

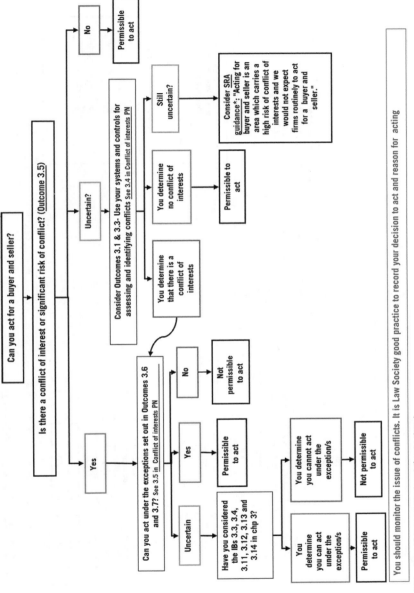

Can you act for a buyer and seller?

Is there a conflict of interest or significant risk of conflict? (Outcome 3.5)

No → Permissible to act

Uncertain? → Consider Outcomes 3.1 & 3.3- Use your systems and controls for assessing and identifying conflicts See 3.4 in Conflict of interests PN

Still uncertain? → Consider SRA guidance*: "Acting for buyer and seller is an area which carries a high risk of conflict of interests and we would not expect firms routinely to act for a buyer and seller."

You determine no conflict of interests → Permissible to act

You determine that there is a conflict of interests

Yes → Can you act under the exceptions set out in Outcomes 3.6 and 3.7? See 3.5 in Conflict of interests PN

No → Not permissible to act

Yes → Permissible to act

Uncertain → Have you considered the IBs 3.3, 3.4, 3.11, 3.12, 3.13 and 3.14 in chp 3?

You determine you can act under the exception/s → Permissible to act

You determine you cannot act under the exception/s → Not permissible to act

You should monitor the issue of conflicts. It is Law Society good practice to record your decision to act and reason for acting

*SRA guidance 'Outcomes focused regulation at a glance'
IB- Indicative behaviours (non-mandatory) in the Code of Conduct 2011

195

LENDER AND BORROWER

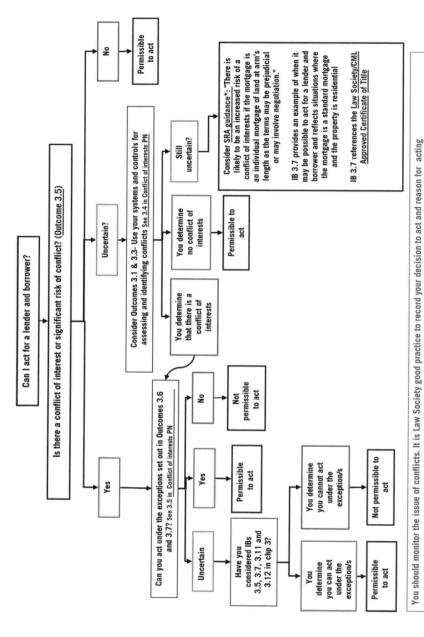

Can I act for a lender and borrower?

Is there a conflict of interest or significant risk of conflict? (Outcome 3.5)

No → Permissible to act

Uncertain? → Consider Outcomes 3.1 & 3.3- Use your systems and controls for assessing and identifying conflicts See 3.4 in Conflict of interests PN

- You determine that there is a conflict of interests
- You determine no conflict of interests → Permissible to act

Still uncertain? → Consider SRA guidance*: "There is likely to be an increased risk of a conflict of interests if the mortgage is an individual mortgage of land at arm's length as the terms may be prejudicial or may involve negotiation."

IB 3.7 provides an example of when it may be possible to act for a lender and borrower and reflects situations where the mortgage is a standard mortgage and the property is residential

IB 3.7 references the Law Society/CML Approved Certificate of Title

Yes → Can you act under the exceptions set out in Outcomes 3.6 and 3.7? See 3.5 in Conflict of interests PN

- **No** → Not permissible to act
- **Yes** → Permissible to act
- **Uncertain** → Have you considered IBs 3.5, 3.7, 3.11 and 3.12 in chp 3?
  - You determine you can act under the exception/s → Permissible to act
  - You determine you cannot act under the exception/s → Not permissible to act

You should monitor the issue of conflicts. It is Law Society good practice to record your decision to act and reason for acting

*SRA guidance 'Outcomes focused regulation at a glance'
IB- Indicative behaviours (non-mandatory) in the Code of Conduct 2011

APPENDIX 13

Dreamvar: an informative and case summary[1]

The Law Society has prepared an informative and case summary following the Court of Appeal decision in *Dreamvar v Mishcon de Reya* ('Dreamvar') and *P&P Property Limited v Owen White & Catlin LLP* ('P&P'). The case involved the liability of solicitors in cases of identity fraud.

SUMMARY OF THE DREAMVAR CASE

1. On 15 May 2018, the Court of Appeal handed down its decision in (1) *P&P Property Ltd v Owen White & Catlin LLP* and *Crownvent Ltd and (2) Dreamvar (UK) Ltd v Mishcon De Reya and Mary Monson Solicitors* [2018] EWCA Civ 1082. There were some similar facts in both cases, so the appeals were heard together. (It is not yet known whether there will be an appeal to the Supreme Court.)
2. Both cases involved the liability of solicitors in cases of identity fraud. Fraudulent people posed as sellers of properties in London both worth about £1m. They instructed estate agents and genuine buyers were found. The fraudulent sellers and the genuine buyers each instructed their own solicitors.
3. The sales went ahead – contracts were exchanged, and completion of the sales and purchases took place on the basis of the provisions of the Law Society Code for Completion 2011 (the Code). After completion, but before registration at HM Land Registry, the frauds were discovered.
4. As completion had not in fact been effected the buyers were entitled to recover the purchase monies paid over on completion, however the fraudsters and the purchase monies had disappeared. The buyers took action to recover the purchase monies by claiming against the seller's solicitors for breach of warranty of authority, breach of trust and breach of undertaking. They also took action against their own solicitors for breach of trust (Dreamvar case).
5. In the Dreamvar case the solicitors instructed by the fraudster seller had not carried out all the identity checks that the circumstances required.

Decision in the High Court

6. In the High Court the buyer's claims against the seller's solicitors were dismissed. In the Dreamvar case, the High Court ruled that Mishcon de Reya had not been negligent and so was not liable in contract or tort but had received money from its buyer client on trust to use it for a genuine completion and so had to bear the losses of the buyer client on a strict liability basis. Even though the firm had not been negligent it was refused relief under the Trustee Act 1925. It was held liable mainly on the basis that it held insurance whereas its clients did not. The result in the High Court was that Mishcon de Reya (as

[1] © The Law Society. Last updated 15 February 2019.

the buyer's solicitors) were held liable even though it was the seller's solicitors who had failed to carry out their obligations under the Money Laundering Regulations 2007.

7. Mishcon de Reya appealed to the Court of Appeal contesting the refusal of relief under the Trustee Act 1925 and contesting the ruling that the fraudulent seller's solicitors had no liability either to Mishcon de Reya or to its buyer client.

The Court of Appeal judgment

8. The Court of Appeal decision in Dreamvar can be summarised as:

(a) Mishcon de Reya had not been negligent and were not liable to their buyer client in contract or tort.

(b) Mishcon de Reya were however liable for breach of trust in parting with the completion money at a non-genuine completion.

(c) the Court of Appeal should not interfere with the first instance judge's decision to refuse relief to Mishcon de Reya under the Trustee Act 1925 and his main reason (that Mishcon de Reya had indemnity insurance) was not plainly wrong (Gloster LJ dissenting).

(d) The fraudster seller's solicitor had no general duty of care to the buyer or the buyer's solicitor and was not liable to the buyer in tort.

(e) The fraudster seller's solicitor was however in breach of the undertaking to the buyer's solicitor implied by the Code for Completion by Post, which as properly interpreted required the seller's solicitor to use the completion money for a genuine completion.

(f) The fraudster seller's solicitor had received the buyer's completion money, via the buyer's solicitor, on trust to use it for a genuine completion and were liable to the buyer for breach of trust. (The fact that the Code requires completion to take place as soon as the seller's solicitor hears that the funds have reached its bank account did not mean that there was no time at which the funds were held on trust for the buyer).

(g) Because of the findings in e. and f. above, Mishcon de Reya were entitled to claim contribution from the fraudster seller's solicitor towards the buyer's claim against Mishcon de Reya.

The case gives rise to a number of difficult practical and legal issues. These require careful and detailed consideration.

We continue to consider the complex implications of the judgment for commercial and residential property transactions.

We are also reviewing the interpretation placed on the Law Society Code for Completion (the Code) and assessing whether and how the Code and other Law Society documents might be amended. Other elements of practice are also being reviewed.

Steps you can take now

- Review your policy for risk assessing transactions, identify the facts that make a matter high risk and make efforts to ensure that you have procedures in place to deal with those risks.

- Review or establish policies about when you might ask seller's solicitors or conveyancers questions, for example, about whether they have carried out their AML investigations. Consider raising questions where there are indicators of potential fraud of the type highlighted in the HM Land Registry/Law Society joint note on Property and Title Fraud. Note: if you raise questions but fail to pursue the responses properly, you may be exposed to additional risk.

- Review or establish policies in relation to how you will answer questions from the buyer's solicitors when acting for a seller.
- Review or develop policies to establish when you should decline to act if you are not confident that the 'seller' is the registered proprietor.
- Ensure that you are aware of and put into practice:

  - Anti-money laundering guidance. This takes into account the 2017 Money Laundering Regulations and provides information about the enhanced due diligence required if you don't meet the client face to face.
  - HM Land Registry: Practice guide 67: evidence of identity; conveyancers. This explains when confirmation of identity or rule 17 identity evidence is required and how it should be given.
  - Property and registration fraud practice note. This is a formal practice note produced jointly by HM Land Registry and the Law Society.
  - Joint property and title fraud advice note. See the examples of the risk factors set out in this note – properties owned for a long time, owned by a sole owner, free from mortgage, urgency of transaction, potential undervalue, limited or conflicting client contact details.

For general information, please contact the Practice Advice Service